Josy,

THE PEAS WERE COLD

THE COLUMNS OF BARRY DAMSKY

Most Sincerely,

Barry Damsky

ISBN: 978-0-692-02123-1

Dedication

In the mid-70's, I showed my writing to my mother's sister, Flo Federman, a reader. She didn't tell me to go be a writer, but I knew I had gotten through to her.

And then in the early 90's, I showed my aging mother, when she was visiting us, a piece I had written. She sat on the side-enclosed porch of our house and when finished, well – her response let me know that I had something, something I could call my own, a gift. Where it would take me, if anywhere, I had not the slightest clue, but it was like a flame was lit deep within me, a flame of hope.

Hope - Hallelujah!

I showed some pieces of my writing to Bill Mudge, my dear friend and then Methodist pastor and was absolutely thrilled at his remarks. A true turning point in my life. Years later, when I wrote the *Boonville Herald* columns, I'd occasionally send him some potential columns I wasn't quite sure of, seeking his advice. He was always remarkably positive about all of them.

My New York theatrical agency boss in the mid 60's, Bobby Brenner, has been privy to my life since then. I'd mail him my columns throughout the years, and when I told him I was going to publish the best of them in this book, he excitedly responded, "You've made my day!" Coming from him, hearing that, meant the world to me.

I want to thank my incredible wife who has patiently witnessed a good portion of what you will read.

She makes me laugh.

I love her so.

Gratefulness to my daughter Melissa and son Deane, precious gifts beyond words.

Special thanks to Cindy Sue Panara for her Herculean editing effort and to Ann Walseman, a pivotal contributor in so many ways.

I would be remiss and a coward were I not to thank my Lord Jesus, who took me from darkness to light. None of this would have been possible without Him. None of it. Nor what is to be.

By all means, be groovin with, *The Peas Were Cold.*

Barry Damsky

Foreword

I absolutely love this book.

I know you're supposed to "love" people and "like" things, but what I love about *The Peas Were Cold* is how it engagingly, inspiringly, and, with great attitude and humor, tells stories about – people!

With columnist Barry Damsky as its main character, in a sense, this book takes you to "life's stage" where he shares stories about the famous and not-so-famous that he's met along the way.

Since 2002, Barry has penned a weekly column for the rural weekly upstate New York newspaper, the *Boonville Herald*. These stories remind us to enjoy every moment of life, relish the love of family and friends, keep dreaming our dreams and to be open to new people and experiences along life's way.

If you're like me, you'll be sure to chuckle, or perhaps find yourself laughing-out-loud. The next moment, you'll find a lump swelling up in your throat, and your heart will feel a tender emotion.

In the over 25 years that I have known Barry, we have shared a similar passion for singing, songwriting and performance. It wasn't until recently that Barry told me he has been document-ing and writing his experiences since the late 1960's because he needed an expressive outlet in addition to all of his other creative pursuits. I think God had been preparing Barry all along to write this book because he is, inherently, a creative person who desires to generously share his "voice" and heart with the rest of us.

Which brings us to this moment – the publishing of *The Peas Were Cold*.

Quite often, it has been mentioned by friends and acquain-tances that Barry should publish a book because he has such interesting stories to tell. They were right.

So, without further ado, I am most honored and humbled to introduce author, storyteller, columnist, singer/songwriter, friend, former theatrical agent and actor, mouse-catcher, Casabubu's friend, husband, father, and Christian – Barry Damsky!

Applause, and, particularly laughter, is permitted at any time as you read *The Peas Were Cold.*

Enjoy!

Ann M. Walseman

Contents

The Boonville Years

Linda Eastman McCartney

(First published submission)
Published in the April 28, 1998 Utica *Observer-Dispatch*

My wife and I were watching TV when the news came crawling at the bottom of the screen that Linda McCartney had died from breast cancer.

It was in the early summer of 1968. I was heading into the home stretch of my first three-year job in New York with a large theatrical agency. Home stretch meaning I was fired and was given some time to find a new job. One of my responsibilities was to make a weekly call to *Record World*, a music publication, to find out what number an artist or group's record was on the pop charts that week. The higher up on the music charts the talent climbed that we represented, the more valuable they became.

Since I was single, I asked my contact at that magazine who he'd recommend dating in the record business. One person he suggested didn't respond; another, Linda Eastman, did.

We made arrangements to have lunch. When Linda walked into my office, she had a flowing beauty about her I had never seen on any female.

We went to a nearby restaurant where we discussed many subjects. She asked me about my job in great detail. She had a simple and earthy quality about her, but it was her inner spirit that was so stunning. She had a pure and fresh outlook on any subject we discussed.

Our lunch went smoothly and all too quickly. She spoke passionately of her photography, specifically her work with the Rolling Stones and the Beatles. I could hardly believe I was talking to someone on such an intimate level about two of the most influential pop musical groups of all time.

Since I knew I'd be leaving my theatrical agency position and although I conveniently left out the part about my being fired, we talked of my desire to enter the area of show business management. A talent manager is intimately involved in all phases of that talent's career. Linda was extremely encouraging about that possibility.

We walked the few blocks to my office and wished each other well, perhaps sensing this was one of those brief encounters in life.

After that lunch date, I called her a couple of times. During our last conversation, she told me she was flying to London the next day and would be there for awhile for her photography.

A few weeks went by and I concluded my last day at the theatrical agency. On the way to my apartment, I had to pass a newsstand. I couldn't help but notice a blaring newspaper headline on one of the New York tabloids, with a big picture of Linda Eastman on its cover, telling one and all she was in England and further, announcing her engagement to Paul McCartney of the Beatles.

Surprise!

I saw Linda two more times after she married. I was living in Los Angeles and had a small theatrical agency. Paul McCartney's band, *Wings*, was playing the big sports arena and I went with a friend. It was the greatest act I'd ever seen. Linda was onstage with the band, playing the keyboard and singing back-up to her husband. I went again three days later on the last night they performed. They were as incredible as the first time I saw them days earlier.

Linda McCartney's death at age 56, prompted sadness for a person I knew for a brief, but impressive, moment. She died too young. What a tragic loss to her husband and family.

May her soul rest in peace.

9/11 Response

Published in the September 16, 2001 Utica *Observer-Dispatch* as a Letter to the Editor

As I stood in the lobby of Utica's St. Luke's Memorial Hospital last Tuesday, the TV hanging from the ceiling in their lobby was being watched by about 15 people. They were viewing the latest wrenching reports from the World Trade Center, along with the two airplane carnages.

I noticed an African-American woman near the wall in the corridor, watching so intently, it propelled me to stop and view what I really didn't want to see. Seeing the reports and playback of both towers being struck made me feel helpless and so sad. As the devastation unfolded, I heard a barely discernible voice in back of me uttering, "Jesus, Jesus."

At first, I thought the person was swearing, but as the TV drama unfolded, I realized her voice was quietly asking for strength from Jesus, and not using His name in vain.

I then heard a faint walking away of that person.

I then asked Jesus for that same strength and peace.

Winnie Said That?

December 14, 2011

Perseverance ... You hear about it as being essential to success. It sure makes sense. *Webster's Dictionary* has this to say about the word persevere: "To persist in any purpose or idea; to strive in spite of difficulties or obstacles".

There's a story that is hard to believe about Winston Churchill, the Prime Minister of England, known for his leadership during the Second World War. That story is that it took him three years to complete eighth grade.

Why?

Because he had difficulty learning English.

Another story about Winston was that he was invited to give the graduation speech at Oxford University, to this day, a most prestigious institution of higher learning.

When he gave the address, he had his usual cigar, cane and top hat. When introduced, the respectful audience rose, giving him a resounding welcome.

In that unmistakable dignity of his, the crowd settled down as he stood before those there that held him in the highest of esteem.

He put his cigar and top hat on the lectern, hesitated, and with his famous authority the world became familiar with, cried out, "Never give up!" Pausing for a short time, he stretched himself, this time shouting, "Never give up!"

He then picked up his cigar, top hat and cane – and left.

Those six words were the sum total of that profound commencement address, probably the shortest speech ever given at any school of higher learning.

Would you guess those brief, yet penetrating words of wisdom, were ever forgotten by all those there?

What was Winston's commencement address message?

Perseverance...

Do only the Winston Churchills of the world have it? Those who persevere more than others... are they the only ones who truly "make it?"

It's hard work, this perseverance business. Blood, sweat and tears – perseverance – all one, right?

I've pretty much written since the mid '60s as a form of self-expression, so no one, publically, saw it – save the Linda McCartney and 9/11 Utica *Observer-Dispatch* pieces – until 11 years ago, when I started writing these columns.

I'm deeply involved in the intricate planning stages of having published – what I would like to think – are the best of those columns, soon to be released in electronic and hard copy book form. The title will be, *The Peas Were Cold.*

When you self-publish, as I'm doing, your chances of success are pretty slim. Not "pretty" slim, I'm told; unbelievably slim.

But if it's "in the cards", or what I believe to be God's will, then anything can happen. One thing is for sure, if I don't do it, there's absolutely no chance of success. I don't want to be rocking on my front porch in years to come remarking to my wife, "I wonder what would have happened, if with some editing, I had put the columns out in book form?"

I keep thinking from time to time about good old Winston and his incisive perseverance lesson at that long ago commencement exercise.

I hope I've learned his lesson, at least with respect to pushing through this column's book idea.

Perseverance, don't fail me now!

The Early Years

I Dwana Go to Camp

May 8, 2002

For several years, my two older brothers had attended Camp Triangle, the Utica (New York) YMCA summer camp at nearby Lake Moraine near Hamilton, New York. So when it came time for me to "come of age" around age 9 or so, I was expected to go as well. I'm not sure why, but I was not thrilled about it.

So I went. Or should I say, they sent me.

I grew up listening to the great comedian Fred Allen, who had a segment on his radio show entitled, *Allen's Alley*, One of the characters was Senator Beauregard Claghorn, who had a funny expression I did a fair job of mimicking at the time.

He would say for the word "friends," what came out sounding like, "Fray-owns," with the accent on the 'Fray.' "Fray-owns," he would say, "and you are my fray-owns," and he'd continue his blustering. So when I imitated him in front of whomever I was saying it to, they laughed …

While at that YMCA camp, when I felt it appropriate, I would imitate that expression as Senator Claghorn did … and it got the laughing results I had grown used to.

One lunch occasion, the director of the camp was in front of everyone explaining the afternoon's events. Instead of listening intently to him as the rest were, I was whispering who knows what to the camper next to me. I then heard my name being called by the director. I looked at him and he said, "Barry, come up here."

Caught!

So I went up, ahhhh … sheepishly.

When there, he turned me around so that I was facing everyone in that large "mess hall." Looking down at me, he said, "What you were talking about to your neighbor must have been pretty important. Why don't you tell us all what it was. We'd like to know."

My mind went blank. I didn't know what to tell him. I forgot what I was talking to "my neighbor" about, and even if I had remembered, it certainly wasn't important enough to tell everybody. I was in trouble. So what was my response? I decided not to say anything, but looked at the floor for help which, incidentally, it didn't give me.

"Well," he said after what seemed an eternity, "I guess you've realized the error of your ways. Do you have anything to say for yourself?"

I don't know what possessed me to say it, but I then responded in my best Senator Claghorn voice, "Fray-owns, no."

The place erupted in hysterics. I really don't think he knew what to do at that point. Here they were – all laughing and clapping – really carrying on. Thank God he let me return to my seat next to my neighbor, whom I don't think I ever said another word to after that, not only in that mess hall, but at any other place. But when you think about it, Senator Claghorn rescued me in my moment of unquestioned need.

I know it's been a long time, but better late than never … thank you Senator Claghorn, wherever you are.

Training for the Indianapolis 500

October 3, 2012

I was 14. My cousin, Donald, was visiting from New York City. He and my older brother, Alan, were shooting baskets on the tree near our garage in Utica.

My father, Hyman, whom my mother addressed as Hy, was watching a Sunday afternoon football game.

I was on our third floor apartment back porch watching the basketball action below.

Our 1949 Buick Roadmaster was parked in the backyard dirt driveway about 20 feet facing our stall of grandpa's two-stall garage.

Alan suddenly ran up the back stairs, took dad's car keys from where we all knew he put them and returned to where the car was parked. He entered the driver's side, started the car, drove it a few feet and then shut it off. He exited the car, proud he could show his cousin in some small way, the results of his newly acquired driver's learner's permit.

He returned upstairs and replaced the keys.

Not to be outdone, a voice deep within me, blared something like, "Hey, how about me? I'm someone!"

I went to where dad's keys were, quietly took them and went downstairs to the outside and with a confidence my brother and cousin couldn't help but notice, entered the Buick. They stopped their basketball activity, more than curious as to what I was up to.

I inserted the key in the ignition, turned it as I had seen my father do so often, starting the car. And it worked!

So far so good.

I put the gear shift into drive as I had also seen him do. The car immediately started rolling toward the garage. I then panicked, not sure if the brake was the accelerator, or the accelerator was the brake, knowing if I chose the wrong one, ahhhh…. "potchy on my tushie" - big time!

The car, in my indecisiveness, was continuing to slowly move forward guided by the dirt ruts that had been built up over time that led to our side of the garage.

The garage doors were closed.

I briefly glanced over to my brother and cousin who were observing me and the slow moving runaway car, both with similar looks on their faces – horror.

The car, as if in slow motion, lazily crackled through our garage doors like a knife through margarine.

And, miracle of miracles, the car came to a halt inside the garage mere inches from the back wall.

I didn't know what to do, but knew it was "curtains" … and not the living room kind.

I heard shouting, and in particular, my mother from the top porch yelling to my father inside, "Hy, Hy, Barry just drove the car through the garage doors!"

My grandfather, who owned our three-story apartment house, who could yell pretty good, was yelling like I never heard him yell before.

I was so scared; all I could think to do was cry.

And cry I did.

Chaos was everywhere.

I dazedly entered my grandparents' first floor apartment and sat in their kitchen next to the refrigerator – wailing.

My father came in, looked at me oddly for a few seconds and left, I suspected, to view the damage to garage and car.

Later, upon looking at the garage doors before they were

replaced, where the car easily muscled its way through, it was as if a giant pair of scissors had sheared the doors horizontally half-way up from the ground.

The car had not a scratch on it prompting later references to it as, "the tank".

And, to this day, if I'm in the presence of my cousin Donald, which is most infrequent, there's a more than decent chance he'll make a reference to the day I drove dad's car through the garage doors.

Brother Alan in front of our garage doors
I'd torpedo 2 years later. 1950

<u>You</u> Get the Bike!

May 22, 2002

It was the summer before I entered high school in Utica. My family rented a camp in Old Forge in the nearby Adirondack Mountains.

I had two close friends, both from Utica. One was Bobby Segaul, a doctor's son, whose brother, father and cousin were doctors. Bobby is a doctor in Plantation, Florida, and owns a winterized camp 20 minutes from Old Forge on Fourth Lake, which he, his wife and family enjoy mostly during the summer months. Generally, I see them at their camp once a year, catching up on all the old gang we knew from Utica.

My other friend, Dick Rizika, had a family camp on a tiny inlet off "The Channel" that leads from Old Forge's pond to the subsequent four lakes.

So the three of us hung around Old Forge a lot that summer. One gorgeous, sunny Adirondack Mountain day, we were congregated on the long dock at the beginning of the pond at Old Forge's beach, where visiting boats tied up, including the long tour boat that daily traveled the four lakes.

Bobby had his red bike with him.

At the end of the long dock, if you gazed down into the water that day, you oddly saw chicken bones at the bottom of the lake. Not that many, but enough. I recall looking at "them" and it was somehow creepy. But there was no question that they weren't anything but chicken bones.

I was slowly riding Bobby's bike on the dock and got the bright idea to drive toward the end of it, pretending I'd drive it into the water. I would of course, stop at the edge, supposedly just in the nick of time. And each time I did it, Bobby and Dick laughed.

My approaches got faster and I'd start the routine further and further back on the dock to get more momentum and maximize the drama. Each time I did it, I would stop closer to the edge of the dock.

The closer I got, the more they laughed.

During my last attempt, I started at the beginning of the dock and pedaled as fast as I could toward the end. I was flying by that time, and when I put on the brakes, the bike skidded from the momentum toward the edge and almost in slow-motion fashion, I sailed over the front of the handlebars … bike, clothes, sneakers, wallet, glasses … all accompanied me as I entered that "chicken-boned" water.

My glasses – which I could see nothing without – happened to be starting their descent. I luckily plucked them out of the water. My two friends were half laughing and fully urging me to dive down and get the bike. Get the bike? All I could think about was how I wanted to distance myself as quickly as possible from those chicken bones. And that didn't include my diving down among them to get the bike.

People suddenly appeared urging me to fetch the bike. One in-sightful bystander suggested Bobby utilize a long, spear-like pole from the tour boat tied by the side of the dock, to fish the bike out with. Bobby took advantage of the suggestion.

I was standing on the dock in a trance-like state, not sure if I should laugh or fall down from chicken-bone fright. I knew I had to go back to my camp and change my clothes and was concerned what I'd tell my mother when she saw me soaked on a sunny Adirondack day.

When I see Bobby Segaul for our one-day summer reunions,

more often than not, he'll at least make a reference to the day I drove his bike off the Old Forge dock.

If he does, in defense of not going down after the bike, it's possible I'd mention the intimidating chicken bones.

Dogs I Have Known

June 5, 2002

Let me say, I grew up with dogs.

Our first one was Spot. I was about seven. He didn't give cars the respect they deserved, and well, you know the rest of the story. That did not deter our family's quest for man's best friend. The veterinarian, who pronounced Spot permanently deleted from mankind because of his car apathy, felt sorry for my crying. He gave us a replacement ... free.

We had him one night. He would walk from one side of the kitchen to the other, and regurgitate, once more proving you get nothing for nothing. We took him back and went full tilt for $5, buying one that had a better digestive disposition. Our creativity knew no bounds in naming him. He had a white tip on his tail, thus the name Tippy.

He lasted about 4 or so years. I think he just got bored with our way of life, for he went out one day and must have heard the expression, "Go West, young man," thinking he was a man. We gave up looking for him after the third year.

Next came Butch. He was pretty cool, and on Friday nights, took his frustrations of life out on Sye, the German Shepherd across the street. Sye had the same distaste for our dog Butch, or Butchie, as my mother used to call him. On Friday nights at about 9:30, they would stage their version of "Bite Out at the OK Corral", for in the middle of the road – again, I am not kidding – Butch and Sye would square off. Their intent? To kill each other.

I've never seen such hatred. We threw water, even milk, on them ... threatening them with baseball bats. On one combative occasion, I got between them, held each by his collar and one bit the tip of my fingernail. I never interceded after that.

When I moved away to New York, my mother had a French Poodle named Tico. When I would come home to visit, I noticed immediately Tico had a higher IQ than mine. Where was he when I took my college entrance exams?

When I subsequently moved out to Los Angeles, after parking my car one morning, I was walking to my theatrical agency office in fashionable Beverly Hills. When walking past an impressive looking house, I noticed in front of it, a massive, and what I thought, friendly–looking brown dog.

I put out my hand to pet it and he must have been confused – thinking my hand was some form of Bitty Bites or whatever they eat – and that dog bit my hand. The owner of the house was a medical doctor. I went to his Beverly Hills office, whereupon he gave me a tetanus shot. "I can't understand it," he said, "He's never done anything like that to anyone."

Lucky me.

I've noticed since then that my policy for possessing a dog has leaned toward the negative direction. I'm not even so crazy about petting dogs that I know are friendly.

So, now you have it.

Oh, I suppose at some future time, a puppy will take my fancy, along with pleadings from some members of my family.

But it will pass.

Believe me.

"OK, who's got my pants?" (Butch) 1956

You Hit It Where?

June 18, 2002

My son Deane and I got up early recently on a Sunday, drove the 35 minutes to Utica from here in Boonville where we live, and took a one-day bus trip to Yankee Stadium to see the New York Yankees play the San Francisco Giants.

It was, indeed, an exciting game, with the Yankees going ahead in the 9th inning and winning the game. Seeing San Francisco's great "home-run machine" Barry Bonds made it even more exciting. The Yankees, unsurprisingly, walked him three times.

We sat 15 rows from the top, between third-base and home plate. The way Yankee Stadium is built, it's steep, so that even though we were that far up, we could see just beautifully above the action. As I sat there, I glanced down to home plate and guessed where my dad and I sat many, many years earlier ... about 25 rows to the left behind home plate.

He and I had gone early, for Dad knew in doing that, we'd be able to see batting practice. I was about nine. As I sat there that day watching a Yankee player taking batting practice, he hit one that went foul, and it suddenly landed about three rows in front of us. Since the game wasn't to start for awhile, no one was around us. Excitedly, my father urged me to hurry and get the ball before anyone else did. Already, there were a couple of people starting to run toward where the ball lay. I excitedly scurried the few rows and scooped it up.

I couldn't believe it. I had a baseball ... hit by a Yankee ... in Yankee Stadium ... in famed New York City!

There wasn't much in life that I could present to my two older brothers that would impress them. But when I showed them

– guardedly – that hallowed baseball, it increased their respect for me to the highest point in my life – thus far – though it was probably for the baseball and not for me. And, I protected that ball as a badge of some kind of honor … that for that moment in my life showed that I was on a more than level playing field with them.

One Friday night, not too long after that, they both came to me explaining they were going to have a small baseball game down the street in front of the high school with some of our neighbor friends. They didn't have a baseball and asked if they could borrow my Yankee one, assuring me they'd take real good care of it. I staunchly refused fearing great harm would befall it. They worked on me as two older brothers knew how to, and after their fervent promises of protection for it, I reluctantly gave in, handing it over.

Not long after that, they both returned with as much sincerity as I'd ever seen them have. My middle brother told me that the ball was accidentally hit through one of the high school windows.

I was crestfallen. I no longer had the equalizer with them I had enjoyed for such a brief moment in my life.

As I sat there in Yankee Stadium two Sundays ago with Deane – among 55,000 plus – I briefly thought about that long ago day my father and I were there … and that baseball. I didn't have time to think much more about it, as the drama of the game with my son took my attention. An additional memory of that day was my son and me eating Yankee Stadium hot dogs. I've never forgotten those incredible hot dogs.

How often I've been told to enjoy the time I have with my children because "it goes fast." Deane will be off to college in two years.

Oh my.

Time is so precious.

Say Something – Anything!

July 20, 2002

My teenage son has just embarked on his first summer job at a nearby restaurant where he's a busboy and washes dishes as well.

At the beginning of one summer in our early high school years, two of my friends and I decided we'd try to get a job as waiters for the summer at a large Adirondack Mountain hotel. As the three of us were ushered into a small office, the man in charge of making those types of decisions quietly sat with his head tilted down looking at the desk in front of him, with a most somber look. I figured a tragedy must have happened to him. He didn't speak for an inordinate amount of time. We knew he knew of our presence because we were sitting right in front of him. He acted like we weren't there.

He finally looked up at us, and with what he next said, informed us as to why he was in such a sad and concerned state. He quietly uttered, "The peas were cold."

The peas were cold.

He then asked each of us if we had any experience as waiters. When it was my turn, I ah – stretched the truth – a lot, and told him I had experience at a hotel in the Catskills. I think he knew I didn't, for he didn't ask me what hotel. And, more importantly, didn't hire me or my two friends … who had as much waiter experience as I did.

Many years later, when living in New York and committed to my aspiring acting phase of life, I had a job on weekends as a waiter at a restaurant in Brooklyn Heights. When introduced to the chef, I was casually told by the person who introduced us that the holes in the kitchen ceiling were caused by the chef's dissatisfaction at the time … by his gun. The chef didn't deny the reason for the "holey" ceiling.

He would get a little crazy from time to time if you didn't pick up the food as quickly as he wanted you to, but he didn't bring in the big guns … oops … ehhh … he didn't revert to his "holes-in-the-ceiling" behavior.

I also worked at an east side mid-Manhattan fancy restaurant for a short time. I was paired off with another "wait" person. That person would actually take the order for the meal, and I would serve it. And you were not supposed to eat anything from the kitchen. That was an absolute no-no.

Now, this fancy restaurant had food that – by looking at it – would prompt you to salivate, no matter how hungry you were. And, of course, as the evening progressed, at about eleven at night, you were hungry. And, the key-lime pie that looked good at seven o'clock, looked incredible by 11.

One night – taken by a fit of hunger unsurpassed in my life – I broke the rule of not eating their food. I found myself in some hidden corner stuffing key lime pie as quickly as I could into my mouth. It's been a long time, but not long enough to forget that I got caught.

Another night, at that restaurant, the girl I was working with at 1:30 in the morning, came to me with a look of grave concern on her face. She told me that the customers we had waited on had just left without paying their bill. The rule was that, if that happened, the waiters had to pay the bill. I went home with about 30 cents in my pocket and was lucky to have that.

The maître d' was a classy, pompous sort, who would stand like a colonel with his arms crossed. I did an imitation of him my fellow "wait" persons requested I perform, and that always got a laugh. On one occasion – as I did that – I noticed they weren't laughing. Turning around, with my arms crossed, I saw the maître d' with <u>his</u> arms crossed, looking at me ... hard.

Anyway, I wish my son much luck and success as he faces his summer career as a busboy and dish washer.

My advice to him?

I think I better ... ahhhhh ... hold off on that.

All Because of Pennies

August 6, 2002

Since my mother's sister Flo, lived in New York City, it was common for us to visit her and her family there. The next block up from her apartment was famed Broadway. And I would save my pennies all year for two reasons. One was so that when I was in New York with my parents, I could go to a couple of penny arcades and spend a lot off those pennies they exchanged for nickels, to play the games.

Ah, that bear you shot with a rifle with a circle somewhere around its mid-section ... that you had to hit perfectly as he lumbered on all fours from side to side. And if you hit the circle, the bear would stand up and roar. If you were good enough and hit it before it returned to its normal fours, it would roar again and turn in the opposite direction.

Supposed sharpshooters could have that bear standing up roaring and turning from side to side on its twos until the game ended. And, of course, the more you hit him in that circle, the more points you scored. I was never that good. Maybe two or three times I'd have Old Grizzly standing up "a roaring and a turning."

The true attraction that enthralled me was a recording booth that offered you the opportunity to record what you wanted, and you ended up with a record of it. The one time I did it, at the age of eight or nine, I chose to record Frankie Laine's then popular song, "That Lucky Old Sun." I don't know what it was about the song, but I loved it.

Blues in its own way.

The song told how difficult life was for this guy who worked like a devil for his pay, and how he wanted the Lord above to send him down a cloud with a silver lining. But it was that lucky old sun that he was most jealous of because all it had to do was roll around heaven all day.

My parents would occasionally take us to the Catskills in the summer for a family weekly vacation. Metropolitan and surrounding New Yorkers flocked there as it was a summer haven close to New York City. We – from Utica – were heavily outnumbered by New Yorkers. In that sense, it was like being a minority.

One Concord Resort Hotel night, in their vast lobby, was a grand piano with a seasoned piano player who took requests encouraging those there to sing along. I was about nine. It seems that everything I ever did in my young life centered around when I was eight or nine. I must have been one busy young fella.

Anyway, the piano guy gave the go-ahead for my father to sing a song that everybody seemed to appreciate. Dad was quite a good singer. After he had finished, dad suggested to the piano player that I sing a song. The piano player somewhat hesitatingly approved his request, so I complied with the song, "I Can't Give You Anything But Love, Baby." At the end, everybody clapped and that hardened piano player was very encouraging in his remarks to me. I especially liked the clapping.

The Concord also had a gigantic nightclub that held a lot of people where, nightly, major talent appeared for all the guests to enjoy. One night was an amateur talent night. My father stood up there on that large stage in front of all those people and sang, "Peg O' My Heart". And he won! Utica beat out New York!

The other reason I saved my pennies all year long was, when at the Concord, I'd get to ride their horses. The first time I was on one, the couple of other riders I was with galloped, so my horse galloped. I held on to the horn on that saddle for dear life, greatly fearing I'd fall off. I didn't and it was never quite as hard or scary after that.

When I first moved to Boonville, one weekend day, I raced Cindy Lee around the Boonville Fair racetrack. That was like a dream come true coming down that home stretch, and I was winning ... until my horse stumbled on a hole. We didn't fall down, but it was enough for me to lose the race. Even though I didn't win, it was a glorious experience.

Amazing what pennies can do.

L - R, Myself, older brothers Alan and Michael,
at the Concord Resort Hotel in Kiamesha Lake, New York, 1949

Just One Second, Doc

August 14, 2002

I was a freshman in high school at Utica Free Academy. With two older brothers, I was always trying to "catch up." Probably still am ...

My oldest brother, Michael, was in college. One winter Sunday, my older brother, Alan, announced at lunch that he was going to go skiing at the ski tow a block away from our house.

Alan asked me if I wanted to accompany him. I had never skied before, and not having skis, called my friend who did. He told me I could borrow his, but warned me about them not having safety bindings. He went on to patiently explain that if you had safety bindings, when you fell, your skis would come off. His wouldn't do that.

Did that stop me? As they would say in Russia "nyet", which as you may guess, means, "You said you didn't care, you big dope!"

So, to the slopes of mid-Utica my brother and I went. We skied the entire afternoon. I did very well. No problems.

At supper that night, Alan announced he was returning to the nearby slopes to ski under their lights. Not only did it sound rather dramatic, but more importantly – not to be outdone – I said I would go as well.

My father then said to me, "Didn't you have enough this afternoon?"

My father had insight. And so, spurred on by brotherly affection, competitiveness and much against my father's advice, I went skiing with Alan.

And it was great. In fact, I was so encouraged by how quickly I had caught on; I even attempted to ski down the most challenging part of the slope I had avoided up to that point. It was the steepest part, and you had to be really good to go down it, which based on my progress, I felt I could do.

Besides, my brother had gone down it. What else do you need to know?

So down I went.

I recall going down that hill at what seemed like 400 miles an hour, and in fact, made it to the bottom ... whereupon, I got insecure and tripped over – I really don't know what, if anything – probably a breath ...

And, down I went, tumbling a goodly amount at a respectable speed and distance. When I looked up, several people came up to me, all impressed with the spill they had seen me take. Someone found my glasses that were miraculously intact. I stood up and my right foot hurt.

Someone said, "Maybe he broke his leg." I walked a few feet, and although it hurt, I was able to do it. Another, who sounded like he knew what he was talking about said, "If he had a broken leg, he wouldn't be able to walk on it like that." I was relieved to hear that. Someone else suggested I be taken to our car by a toboggan that suddenly appeared. I didn't argue.

When my brother brought me home, limping, I'll just say I've seen my father happier.

Just to "be sure," they took me to Faxton Hospital a block away. They, of course, x-rayed my leg, and afterwards, our family doctor came in where I was lying. He mentioned that the x-rays showed I had a fractured leg.

As he was walking out of the room, I thanked him for coming and told him how relieved I was that I didn't break my leg.

He stopped, looked at me soberly, and said, "What do you

think a fracture is"? It was only then that I realized the answer to his incisive question.

So I learned three things that day.

1. The importance of safety bindings on skis.
2. What a fracture is, and
3. Papa knows best.

A Scholarship I'll Never Get

October 1, 2003

Pick a season of the year and it has its accompanying sports attached to it. Like right about now, it's football.

One Sunday, my Utica high school fraternity played a team whose players were one step below the high school varsity level. That should have been our first clue.

I was the quarterback for our team. At half time I was pleading with my fellow players to quit because the score was 35 to nothing. Guess who had the nothing? I'll give you a clue. It wasn't them.

"Quit? You can't do that!" one player protested.

"Why not?" I squabbled. "I'm the quarterback ... they're killing me!"

Another fumed, "Quitters never win!"

I then thrust deep down into my arsenal of debating choices, deciding on, "Fine, you go be the quarterback!"

No one said a word.

Unfortunately, it was only a momentary debating success for we did, in fact, play the second half. Surprisingly, my proclivity for prophecy showed remarkable insight, as the score ended up being 65 to nothing. You could say from that game alone, I had a reputation as a quarterback.

While in high school in a game played just between the guys in our fraternity, one player on the opposite team was tall and very sturdily built ... as in "bull."

At one point in the game, I was running with the football and somehow had eluded everyone with only one member of the

33

opposing team between a touchdown and myself.

That one person?

"Dee bull."

I was about 5' 7" at the time, 135 pounds, and he was over six feet and much heavier than me. But I had a secret weapon. I was able to fake people out. That is, I was able to pretend to go one way, and at the last moment, when that person was going for me, I'd suddenly change directions and run around him.

I was convinced I could do that with "dee bull."

It flashed through my mind that I would try to "fight fire with fire." Yes, I'd go right at him with power … bowl him right over … be a real man. Never mind this faking business.

So I did. I ran right at him. Did I get through him to make the touchdown? I can only liken it to running into a tiny portion of the Great Wall of China. Fortunately, all that ended up being hurt ... was my ego.

So, in this new football season, on those occasions I'm able to sit by the TV and safely watch those brave physical souls go at each other, there's a certain amount of safety I take pleasure in from my couch.

By the way, I saw "dee bull" a few years ago. I asked him if he remembered my attempt at going through him that long ago football day. He said, "Yes."

I winced when he said it.

Think I'll go watch TV. Maybe there's a football game on.

"Oy!"

January 28, 2004

With the several cold snaps we've been experiencing as of late, they've triggered me to recall "cold" stories. One happened while growing up in Utica.

My uncle owned the Lincoln Theatre in west Utica, about 20 walking minutes from where we lived. As we grew up, my two older brothers and our selected neighbor friends would attend that theatre mostly on Saturday afternoons.

The ticket takers generally knew us. When we went in, my oldest brother Michael, leading us all, would point to the person in back of him, generally my middle brother, Alan. That signaled the ticket taker that it was all right to let him in as well. Alan would then point to the next in line – me – and I would then, in turn, point to those who followed me and say one word as I had been instructed, "cousins."

The truth? Good friends, yes. Cousins? Ahhhh ... no.

They usually consisted of two brothers of a family who lived across the street from us. Or, if it wasn't them, it was a couple of other neighbor friends, or frequently, the entire combination. We, or in this case, I, was stretching it to include, with my pointing, anyone else who was in our family. My uncle, who had to know what was going on, never said a word to us. That, in retrospect, was pretty cool of him.

Since the movies on the weekends were different from those during the week, we would occasionally go on weekday nights, depending on the importance of the picture being shown. That was always a unique experience as, on Wednesday nights as a promotion, the theatre gave away kitchen plates to lucky ticket holders. We never won because we never bought any tickets.

One memorable mid-winter weeknight, my brother Alan and I went to the Lincoln to see Kirk Douglas in *Champion*. Kirk played a boxer, with enough boxing scenes to have made its impression on us.

Apparently, so imprinted with potential boxing greatness after having seen Kirk do such an inspiring acting job, my brother and I jabbed and feinted with each other as we wended our way home. We also pounded each other on the arms ... to us, a manly sign of courage and honor. And, on that night, when my brother punched me on the arm, because of the severe winter cold, those blows hurt like never before.

I once boxed a very short round in eighth grade with Lyle Zysk, in his cellar, replete with boxing gloves. His father, who had experience in that area, taught him well.

Lyle's first punch to my head got more than my immediate attention. The second one, shortly thereafter, told me if I was smart and wanted to live a full and useful life, I should quit immediately ... which, I'm pleased to say, I did.

It was one of the more intelligent decisions of my life.

A couple of cold snaps ago here in Boonville, our thermometer read 30 below. That's very cold by anyone's standards. But not as cold as it seemed on that long ago, sparring night when my brother pounded me on the arm on the way home from the Lincoln Theatre.

Stay warm.

And if you're tempted to go see a boxing movie on a winter night with your siblings, take the car.

With a heater.

That works.

I Flunked? You Don't Say!

July 13, 2005

At a recent high school reunion, some of us talked about military service. I was asked what my history was, and I gladly filled them in.

In my junior year in high school in Utica, I joined the six month Army Reserve program. I went to basic training at Fort Dix, New Jersey, was a clerk-typist for the remainder of the six months active duty there, and for a total of 5 ½ years, went to summer camp at various army bases. I did all of this while attending weekly reserve meetings.

The unit I was based out of, while in Utica, was an engineering company with a "Dump Truck" tagged to its name. I was in my third year of having attended weekly reserve meetings, when at one of them, my name was called.

The sergeant told me that I was one of the only soldiers in the entire company who didn't have his truck driver's license. And, to correct that – right then and there – I was to take a road test to see if I could pass it. I panicked because I didn't know how to drive a truck; good grounds, I thought, for concern.

Reluctantly climbing up – and I do mean up – to the front seat of what seemed like the Queen Mary on wheels, I was amazed by the dashboard of dials and general strangeness.

I don't know how I started that massive truck, and I found myself driving up the well-traveled road. The diagram on the dashboard told me there was – something like – twelve forward gears. As I was driving and shifting, I didn't know if I was in second gear, twelfth or anywhere in between. Arriving at an intersection, the instructor – with no patience in his voice – told me (well, more like bellowed) – "turn right!" About a minute later, he shouted that I pull over to the side of the road.

When stopped, he wailed, "Soldier, do you want to know if you passed this road test"?

Fearing the worst, I choked "sure" with the worst case scenario being that I passed.

Drawing a huge X through my test he was writing on, he hollered, "You flunked! And do you want to know why you flunked"?

I couldn't think of anything to say except, "Please."

He then stated with great pride, "You didn't shift properly, you didn't pay attention to the speed limit, you didn't signal properly and you were in the wrong gears."

I tried acting as if I was highly disappointed in having flunked, but was inwardly joyful knowing I wouldn't be transporting troops in a truck I didn't know how to drive.

In the remaining years I had to fulfill the couple of weeks of Army summer camp, I was relegated to being a driver's assistant. That meant my main duty was to stand in back of the truck where the driver could see me from his side-view mirror. When he wanted to back up, I signaled if it was all right for him do that. In those instances, I must admit, my fantasy wasn't, "Today, a driver's assistant, tomorrow a Five-Star General."

At my recent high school reunion, where I told this story, someone remarked how I should write a column about it.

Maybe.

Fool That I Am

June 13, 2007

We all know how spring – in all its beauty – has finally arrived
... late.

But late or not, it's been – oh – so glorious. Even though
calendar-wise it has arrived, weather-wise it didn't seem like it
would ever come.

A sure sign of spring here in Boonville are the motorcyclists that
drive by our house. We're on a state road that connects Boonville to
nearby Rome. So we hear them roar by, particularly on weekends,
sometimes so many of them at once, the earth almost trembles.

When I was going to Utica College, one of my friends who
also attended there, decided she wanted to buy a motorcycle. We
heard of one for sale by a student at nearby Hamilton College, and
made arrangements to see it.

One of my close buddies had a British-made Triumph motorcycle when he lived in the Los Angeles area. He told me so often
how "freeing" it was to ride one. He explained how you shift up
and down with your right foot and coordinate it with your right
hand on the handlebar shift. And I understood it. So when the
Hamilton College opportunity presented itself and the motorcycle
was a Triumph, well – that's all we had to hear.

We met the student who owned it on the Hamilton College
campus. There it stood ... and I really didn't know what I was
looking at. Its young owner started it and looked at me, asking if I
wanted to try it – he didn't know I had never been on one before.

Any level-headed human would have said, "No, I don't know
how to drive one."

And that certainly would have showed that I had some wisdom – perhaps not beyond my 21 or so years I was at the time – but at least a start in the right direction.

So what did I do? I got on it and by intellect, drove up the steep road about a hundred yards, shifting as it was explained to me so many times by my buddy, surprised it was as easy to do as it was.

After driving back down the road to where the three of them were, the purchase was made. Although not my own, suddenly there was a motorcycle in my life. It didn't take long – like immediately – for me to experience the freedom that other drivers speak of.

All the while, I had heard from so many that sooner or later, if I continued to drive it, something would happen.

Like an accident.

I drove it one time with a friend of my older brother's seated in back of me. I turned a corner in the middle of Utica and there was sand on the road. The motorcycle shifted and wobbled. It was a miracle to this day nothing happened – I mean miracle.

My nephew had a motorcycle years later and was most logical in his communication when you'd tell him your fear of the possibility he'd have an accident. He would articulate in great detail against that possibility, explaining his most careful defensive driving techniques. He would also describe the correct riding apparel he wore in doing so, and you couldn't help but feel he had a great grip on it.

I don't remember exactly what happened, but the result was that one time while riding it, he hurt his leg. Not enough to have residual results to this day, but enough for him to shortly, thereafter, discontinue driving it anymore.

So, as this fleeting spring slides into next week's arrival of the crown jewel of summer, enjoy it all to the fullest. And no matter what you drive – do not "throw caution to the wind."

Like some guy I know.

Very, very well.

I ... I Just Don't Know

October 19, 2011

I heard my name called to come to her desk. When there, the teacher told me to identify the numbers she would write on a piece of paper.

I was in kindergarten.

In pencil, she wrote a number on a white sheet of paper, asking, "What number is that?"

I was baffled. It certainly didn't look like any of the numbers on my Uncle Max's real estate calendar mother and I had practiced from.

She wrote another number, more urgently requesting its identity. It was equally as unrecognizable. She tried one more time with the same sad result.

She jarringly dictated, "Go home and learn your numbers!"

A week later, I was again summoned to her desk with the same unsuccessful and disquieting result. She caustically stated, "I've told you to learn your numbers and you haven't done that! You better learn your numbers!" That afternoon, as we were all leaving to go home, she told me, "You better learn your numbers. I'm going to test you on them tomorrow and God help you if you don't know them."

What kept going through my mind as the day progressed, were her unforgettable words, "God help you."

The next morning, when it was time to leave for school, I hid my toast in one of our kitchen drawers.

As my two older brothers and I started walking up the street to school, I stopped, telling them I forgot my toast and that I would catch up with them.

I retrieved the toast, undetected by my mother.

Three houses up the street from ours was an old long wooden rope factory that extended from our street to the next one over.

I hid beside it.

And waited.

I did that for what I thought was the entire morning. Guessing it was time for lunch, I returned home. As I walked through the door, my mother sternly greeted me with, "Where were you? Your teacher called and said you weren't in school!"

I broke down tearfully confessing I was frightened by the teacher's, "God help you" threat if I didn't learn my numbers.

At the end of the school term, I was handed a note for my parents. When I gave it to my mother, she was dumbstruck, saying, "I don't understand it, I just don't understand it."

When my father came home that night, they both looked at me and spoke in hushed tones. I knew I had somehow done something wrong, but was baffled as to what it was.

The note I gave my mother said I had flunked kindergarten and had to repeat it.

One day, during the second go round of kindergarten, my name was called, along with several others, to go to the nurse's office.

When it was my turn there, I was instructed to put something over one of my eyes and to read the letters from the chart on the wall.

I asked, "What letters?"

I was told, "Start at the top, the one with the biggest letter."

With confusion, I once again asked, "What big letter?"

Someone said, "You mean you can't read that first letter?"

I embarrassingly said, "No."

I was given a note.

Another note!

I went home, sheepishly handing the note to my mother, figuring I was in for another trauma.

Days later, I was taken to an optician who prescribed very thick glasses.

After that, a whole new detailed world opened up to me.

Looking back on that kindergarten experience, the numbers on Uncle Max's calendar were big and bold and the numbers my teacher wrote with her pencil weren't.

Hindsight? Why didn't I say, "I can't see the numbers?"

That's probably why they call it – hindsight.

Cheese It - the Cops!

November 2, 2011

In my last column, I described how I had to repeat kindergarten, for they thought I was stupid because I couldn't read the numbers they wrote in pencil. Later, they found out I just needed glasses. In that column, I mentioned there was a "rope factory", several houses up the street from ours, which I hid next to when I skipped kindergarten that one day.

My cousin from Portland, Maine – my mother's sister's younger son – emailed me the following after reading the column:

"That rope factory, I was told, was a stop for black slaves on the underground railroad."

I emailed the following back to him:

"Yes, cuz, that rope factory held many memories for us. One time, we snuck into it when it was closed, raising and lowering ourselves from a pulley through a trap door from the second to the first floor and back. I was just scared we'd get caught, which would have severely taken away from the excitement of "the ride".

We would walk from our street through that rope factory to the next street, and if coming from the other side of course, in reverse. The two gentlemen who ran the factory knew us and let us do that. One, named Tim, was a quiet sort.

In an adjoining house lived a third man, who managed the rope factory. There were plum trees in his yard. In late summer, we would sneak into that yard and eat the sweetest plums on earth.

The rope factory had a certain musty smell to it I can still conjure up in my mind.

At one end of the building, one of the men would turn, by hand, a steel-wheeled circular contraption that had strands of rope attached to it. The strands would twist all the way to the other end of the building where the other man signaled him when the twisting was complete. That's how they made rope.

An apartment house has since been built at that location, and in doing so, history was obliterated. Yes, slaves from the south were snuck through there. Amazing history right there in Utica, New York, three houses from where we lived.

As I hid next to that rope factory that long ago kindergarten "skipped school" day – when I decided to go home thinking it was around noontime and everyone would be coming home for lunch – I thought I'd be just ahead of my brothers.

When I got home, my mother was not happy with me, having been called by my teacher as to my whereabouts. It was only about 10 o'clock in the morning. So much for my perception of time … at least, then.

It was the teacher's threat of "God help you" if I didn't learn my numbers that got me to skip school that day. And, with my vivid imagination, I conveniently blocked what might have happened had I gone to school that day and not known my numbers. Yet, knowing deep down because mother and I had practiced them – I knew them. Go figure.

I just needed glasses.

I was called "four eyes" a handful of times, learning it was an insult that never did make sense to me. I even remember one of the person's names who called me that. He lived in a house the next street over, and he invited me to visit him in his house once in the winter. The house didn't have much furniture and was conspicuously cold. I saw his obituary in the Utica paper about a dozen years ago.

He died young.

At least I'm still here. I'm not quite sure what the answer, if any, is up with that.

Just grateful I'm here.

Hope all is well, cuz.

With love,

Barry"

New York City

Stella! Stella!

(First published *Boonville Herald* column)
January 9, 2002

When I took my first acting class in New York back in the late '60s, the teacher, Katharine Sergava, a former ballet dancer, told us she was going to ask us to stand and tell us all what our reasons were for taking the class. The only thing I could think of was, "Oy!"

Looking back on that panicky moment, it may have been divine intervention that I found myself in the back row, for it gave me time to think of an answer I had not the slightest clue to. Various reasons from the students were systematically given, ranging from wanting to be a star, to the answer of boredom.

When one said, "for self-expression," it was at that moment I understood why I was not only there, but also why I was doing some of the things I was doing in my life. I guess it was a sort of an epiphany, a fancy word for "Boing!"

Self-expression – wow – it hit me like a thunderbolt. I told myself, "That's it! That's the reason for my behavior!"

So not only did I have an answer to Katharine's question, albeit not original, but it was the reason I've sung all the years I have, played the guitar and piano and – above all – why I have written since the '60s.

Self-expression ... Whew! What a relief to know!

I also told that long ago first acting class how, when I was about seven years old, I appeared in our Jewish synagogue's Sunday School Purim play in Utica. I had one line to memorize and drove my family a bit wacky making sure I knew it.

About 15 of us stood on that stage, and one by one, took a step forward and delivered our respective lines. My oldest brother, Michael, was the first and tallest, and I, the last and smallest. At the proper moment, I took my obligatory step forward and proclaimed, "Thank you all for listening to us. When peace comes tomorrow, we'll all have a Schnapps." For the record, the *American College Dictionary* reads, "Schnapps: any spirituous liquor." When I said it, the place went wild with laughter and clapped vigorously. I stepped back, but they requested I do it again, which I obliged.

After telling that story in that first acting class, Katharine then lightly asked me, "That's when you were bitten by the acting bug?" I wasn't exactly sure what she meant, but not knowing what else to do, I nodded.

So here I am, 32 years later, continuing to "let it out" by writing this column which, by the way, I'll be writing every other week. The reason for that is because the new owner of this newspaper, Joe Kelly, asked me to.

May I please be so pubic as to say, "Joe, don't ask me any questions in front of anybody, I can't always be in the back."

It Ain't Me Babe

March 27, 2002

In the March 7th Utica *Observer-Dispatch* was a feature article on Cher and how she continues to be successful in her show business career.

After Utica College, I was working for a New York theatrical agency in their television department. The agency had a daily print service they subscribed to which listed celebrities who were in town, for how long, and where they were staying. That kind of information was invaluable, as one of an agent's duties was to sign new clients to the firm for exclusive representation. The department I was a part of was responsible for putting our agency's clients on TV programs like the *Ed Sullivan*, the *Tonight Show* and the *Merv Griffin Show*, all perfect for Sonny & Cher.

One day, I noticed that Sonny & Cher were included on that daily celebrity service list. I went to one of my fellow agent friends, Alfie Schweitzman, whose main duties were placing our agency's acts in colleges and clubs in the New York and Long Island areas. I excitedly suggested to him we try to get to Sonny & Cher, with the intention of both of us signing the act to our agency. His eyes got very wide and he smiled an infectious smile that silently told me his answer. When excited about something, Alfie had an enthusiasm that was absolutely irresistible.

Sonny & Cher's record, "I've Got You Babe," had been a smashing success. Their latest, "The Beat Goes On", was racing up the record charts. There was no question that they were well on their way to becoming a giant act.

We called the hotel they were staying at, asked for Sonny, and, sure enough, he answered. Just getting through to him like that was very unusual, as "stars" of his nature are so well insulated.

After briefly explaining who we represented, he consented to see us. Growing up in a city like Utica most people were unfamiliar with, and here I was going to meet, Sonny & Cher. Unbelievable! When we went to see them, their hotel suite had a staircase I had never seen in any hotel room before or since.

Sonny was so easy to talk with – just a wonderfully sincere guy who happened to be a pop superstar. We told him that we would like to represent him and Cher for college concerts, the night club area and television.

He told us he knew and respected our agency and that he would possibly consider our firm representing them in the area of motion pictures ... lending us some film they had on themselves to show to our film people.

Suddenly, I heard her unmistakable voice exclaiming, "Sonny, I've got something in my eye. I just can't get it out!" Turning to where it came from – descending from the staircase – was the then 19-year-old Cher. Sonny introduced us and she proceeded to frustratingly tell him how she couldn't get out whatever she had in her eye. With great patience and concern, Sonny suggested she pull her lid over her eye, to no avail. I couldn't believe what I was witnessing.

By this time, Cher was so uncomfortable, she urged Sonny to take her to an eye doctor. He agreed and apologized to us that they had to cut our meeting short, ... and, to let them know of our firm's possible interest in their film acting abilities.

Our firm had a formidable motion picture department. Alfie and I knew we had to get somebody high up in that department to be as excited about Sonny & Cher for motion pictures as we were for our areas. If that happened, we still had to convince Sonny & Cher to sign with our agency. With that scenario, we had a chance.

We excitedly passed on Sonny & Cher's film to the head of our film department, a female "spitfire." After viewing that film, she showed no interest, for it didn't show Cher's acting abilities it subsequently took years for her to develop.

Sonny & Cher obviously showed musical comedic brilliance in their subsequent television shows years later, but at that moment, didn't meet the standards of our firm's motion picture department. No amount of attempted spirited enthusiasm on Alfie's and my part – that they were a superstar recording act – could change our film people's minds. Their decision to pass on them was final.

Alfie and I were numbed by their decision, not because we didn't agree Sonny & Cher didn't have the acting abilities any truly professional agency would have demanded to be able to sell them as dramatic actors, but losing them to our respective areas, well – close but no cigar. For us, it was like giving away a miracle that comes perhaps once in one's theatrical agency lifetime.

Alfie called Sonny and told him our agency was most interested in representing them in our areas, but that, thus far, the film department wouldn't commit to them.

So the Utica *Observer-Dispatch* writes about Cher all these years later … and, how her success has withstood the hands of time … how popular – particularly with young people – she continues to be. She's a real classic show biz survivor.

As you may have guessed, Alfie and I didn't sign the act.

I can see now what I couldn't – and rightly so – see then.

Everything in its own time.

Feline Slavery

April 10, 2002

Funny thing about writing a column ... when I start out writing what I thought I'd like to write about, it ends up being something altogether different. Let me pick a subject and see if it doesn't end up somewhere else.

A subject ... let's see ... dogs ... there's a good one. Everybody likes dogs, except when they bark when they shouldn't. Like at three a.m. Not good. In fact, it stirs feelings and thoughts you never thought possible, like "Premature Demise." We'll leave that one alone. Say they bark at four thirty in the afternoon – at what appears to be nothing – is that acceptable?

As Joan Rivers would say, "Please ..."

Now, cats on the other hand have, of course, their legion of proponents declaring, "They have a mind of their own," and of course the obligatory, "They're so clean."

I subleased my New York apartment one summer, and upon returning, found the person I leased it to, forgot something. And when I tried to contact her to tell her she left that something at my apartment ... and would she please come pick up that something ... well, let's just say it fell on deaf ears.

That "something", I later named "Tutty." Yup, her cat.

Yeah, 'her' cat that turned into, 'my' cat. I know I shouldn't say this, but at times, I wanted to kill her – the cat. But – rest assured – I didn't. I didn't even abuse her. I was as she wanted me to be ... her slave.

I recall standing in line at the supermarket, with four containers of yogurt for me and 16 cans of cat food for ... guess who? Do you glimpse where my priorities were?

I will say – as they go – Tutty was a beautiful cat. And she knew it. She would sit on my desk, as if she were the queen of the universe.

I would awake in the morning, sensing I was being beckoned, and sure enough – upon opening my eyes – there, I'd say not even 20 inches away from my view, sat Tutty ... in that imperial-looking way ... silently saying, "Feed me, you fool." And every time, although not entirely thrilled about it, I did.

I was in bondage to her ... a slave to a cat ... I questioned my very life existence as to its purpose because of it.

And if that wasn't enough, I was given a baby male kitten I named Timmy. The kitten was given to me by a friend ... thinking it would be a good companion to Tutty. And indeed, he was. In fact about a year later, they were so "companionable," Tutty had her first of two litters from Timmy. From their "union" emerged a family of six.

You know how it's normal to wait five to six weeks before you can give kittens away? In those six weeks, I had eight cats parading around my one-bedroom apartment. They were everywhere. Oh, I know I will stiffen the backs of you cat loving devotees out there, and, all I can say to that is ... you go live in a one bedroom apartment in New York City with eight cats.

Wait a minute ... I started out talking about dogs. Other than the barking, I never really got into it. It could be said that barking covered the whole thing. Yes, there's more. But not now. Maybe never.

See, I started out with one thing, dogs ... and ended up with another.

Is a dog that different from a cat?

If Tutty could voice her opinion on that, my guess would be she'd say, "Please ..."

Run the Projection Machine?
Shoot Me Now!

March 5, 2003

I just read about an HBO TV film documentary that is going to be produced. It's based on a book just published entitled, *The Mailroom: Hollywood History from the Bottom Up* by David Rensin.

The book is a collection of Hollywood talent agency mailroom stories. Since I was one of those guys who started in the mailroom of a New York talent agency after Utica College, it got me to thinking about those days.

One late afternoon, I was picking up the mail from each agent's desk. It was about five thirty p.m. and mostly everyone had left for the day.

As I approached a secretary's desk, there sat a man with glasses who looked the opposite of sophisticated, who gruffly asked me for a phone book.

I thought, "Who does this schleppy-looking man think he is? Is he a bum? Did he wander in the building and happen to get off on our floor, slip in and just start demanding things"?

Old golden tongue here then asked, "Did you just get off the elevator?"

He looked at me hard and with obvious annoyance said, "I'm Arthur Miller."

And it was then that I realized this man was the former husband of Marilyn Monroe and author of numerous plays, the least of which was the classic, *Death of a Salesman.*

"Oh, Mr. Miller," I stumblingly choked. "I'll get you that telephone book ... hold on."

And I got him one, just shy of Superman speed.

One Saturday morning, I had to work. You never knew what
you'd have to do, but someone from the mailroom was requested
to be there.

Up to that point, I was shown how to use their 16mm film projector. I noticed that most of the mailroom guys had no problem
running it. You threaded the film a certain way, and if you did it
correctly, when you switched the projector on, it worked quietly
and smoothly. When they showed me how to do it, when I tried it,
it never worked like it did for them. Instead, it made a snapping
sound with no picture coming out.

The Saturday I worked, the vice president of the firm came in
the mailroom and asked me to set up the projector to see the pilot
of *Get Smart* starring Don Adams. A pilot is the example, and in
many instances, the first show of a TV series. When I went in to
the projection room to set it up, an executive of the show yelled,
"Hurry up!" Hurry up!"

I thought, "Why would I hurry to my own execution?"

So, I threaded the film as best I could, and when I turned it on,
I prayed it would work.

Apparently, I had recently sinned.

Not only were my prayers not answered as I listened to the
dreaded click-click-click sound with nothing coming out of the
projector, but adding to my woes, I clearly heard the executive
of the show, with renewed passion, ranting at me to, "Hurry up"!

So, with instant acquired perspiration, I tried again.

You guessed it! The same clickety-click, and to make matters
worse, a piece of the film snapped off!

I knew I was dangerously close to dropping dead.

The executive stormed into the projection room and seeing

me with a piece of his only pilot in my hand, launched into a record level of questionable "street" verbiage, the likes of which I'm not quite sure I previously ever heard.

As it happened, the next week I also had to work a Saturday, and the vice president called me into his office. I was sure it was to fire me.

He told me how much he appreciated how hard all of us in the mailroom worked and for me not to take what had happened the previous week too seriously.

It was then that I personally realized what a miracle was.

When that HBO special on mailroom stories comes out on television, I'll be anxious to see it. I hope I'll be able to view it without breaking out in hives.

You Call That an Introduction?

February 9, 2005

After 'getting out' of the mailroom at the New York theatrical agency, my duties in their television department were to place the talent the agency represented on television shows.

The biggest show I represented, before it was moved to Los Angeles, was *The Tonight Show* starring Johnny Carson.

Our agency represented a long list of major established and upcoming talent. It was nothing for me to be at *The Tonight Show* several times a week watching over whomever I had placed on the show.

Before they went on, the talent would gather in what television shows call their "green room," containing a couch, chairs and a television monitor you could watch the show from.

In my dealing with *The Tonight Show*, I didn't come in contact with its emcee. The only time I saw him was on the green room television set when the show was in progress, and of course, when I watched it like everybody else at home.

In one memorable instance, I had placed someone on the show and was walking out of the green room just before the show was about to begin. I glanced around and as I stood there, I couldn't help but notice, standing alone no more than six feet from me, was … Johnny Carson.

I knew enough not to say anything to him as I assumed he was preparing himself to go on the show at any moment. When I glanced at him, he had a sense about him that I've described over the years as, "steel-like." His presence was magnetic, he was incredibly handsome, and was dressed as sophisticatedly as his enormous amount of fans were familiar with. But it was his unmistakable strength of presence that I've never forgotten. I don't know as I've ever seen such strength like that before or since.

One evening, a couple of the agents I worked with were at one of Greenwich Village's nightclubs, The Bitter End. You did that ... you went to clubs in search for the next great talent.

We were sitting at one of their booths with backs high enough so we couldn't see who was sitting on either side of us. Another agent from my firm, who I didn't know was there, surprised me by yelling out to me from a couple of booths away, "Barry Damsky, say hello to Johnny Carson!"

I then heard the familiar voice of Johnny say, "Hello, Barry Damsky."

It was the only introduction I've ever had where I didn't actually see the person I was introduced to, much less shake that person's hand.

I then said the only words I ever said to him, "Hi Johnny."

With his recent death, it brought back so many memories of being at his show all those times and meeting him in that unique way.

That one time I saw him backstage, I can't tell you enough, he was just like polished steel.

There's No Business, Like ...

February 23, 2005

My last column received a surprising response. It was based on my brush with Johnny Carson while in New York City working at the theatrical agency.

After reading that column, a cousin of mine from Colorado wrote me and asked, "Did you get to rub elbows with any other famous or nearly famous people?"

One of the firm's clients was the singer and songwriter Paul Anka. I had caught a glimpse of him one time at the agency. I had never seen such a stunning suit on anyone.

One day, I was given instructions to see that all went smoothly at a new TV show he was appearing on in New York. When I introduced myself to him at the show, he was a breeze to talk to and afterward, we went to his office.

He had a wooden half-moon desk he remarked he had completed many great music deals on. He said that he was going to throw the desk out, pointing to the nicks, scars and general sad shape the top was in.

I asked him if he wouldn't mind if I could have it? So it ended up in my apartment. I sanded the top and applied lemon oil to it and it turned out perfectly.

I recently saw Paul interviewed on the *Larry King Live* television show talking about Johnny Carson. Paul spoke of when *The Tonight Show* accepted his song as their theme song and how he gave Johnny half the song's royalties. He further mentioned that he and Johnny each received something like $200,000 a year in royalties.

Unbelievable.

I placed the aging actress Tallulah Bankhead on *The Tonight Show*. I had to go to her apartment in the middle of the city to explain all the details leading up to the show. That included me picking her up with the limo the show provided. By the way, one of Tallulah's more memorable quotes was, "I'm as pure as the driven slush."

One early evening, I was showing a visiting friend of mine from my Utica College days, the backstage area at *The Tonight Show*. Bobby Kennedy was one of the guests, and before going on, he walked by us deep in hushed conversation with the person he was with. You knew you were around someone important just by his presence alone. I just loved what Bobby was trying to do with his life and when he was assassinated, I had to get out of the city for a couple of days to my middle brother's house in Connecticut. You seek sanity wherever you can get it.

Our firm represented the actress and singer Dinah Shore. She was appearing on a Kraft TV special at the cavernous NBC studios in Brooklyn. I was out there with her for the week she was rehearsing the show.

Dinah did a duet with Ray Charles on his classic hit, "Georgia On My Mind."

One of the incredible moments was when the studio was completely dark except for the dull lights on the grand piano in the middle of the studio. Not many people were around as Ray and Dinah sat on the piano bench together rehearsing the song. The intimacy of them singing it ... well ... I knew I was witnessing something special.

Also appearing on that show, although he wasn't a client of our agency, was the great singer and actor Bobby Darin. Just before Ray and Dinah rehearsed their song, Bobby rehearsed his famous song "Mack the Knife." Even in that huge, darkened, almost empty rehearsal hall, when he sang it, it was electrifying.

Being around talented people in that type of high-powered environment was a true privilege.

Although probably a dream, I have this feeling I'm not through with it.

The early days of writing on the Paul Anka desk, 1968

Should Have Asked Where He Hung Out

April 6, 2005

When I attended the University of Miami in 1957, one of my best friends from Utica, Dick Rizika, was a student there and encouraged me to go there, which I did.

He frequently spoke of a wonderful New York City writer named Jimmy Breslin.

As I sat thumbing through magazines in my wife's hospital room before she was taken for her recent carpal tunnel surgery, I read a reprinted article in the *Better Homes and Gardens* magazine written in 1983. The article, about the Brooklyn Bridge, was authored by the Pulitzer Prize winner Jimmy Breslin. The article was about a Brooklyn policeman, Richard Seaberg, whose beat was the Brooklyn Bridge and how he was called upon to climb it to save people from suicide leaps.

In one instance, Richard was attempting to talk a man out of jumping, who had a glass of beer in his hand. After attempting to dissuade him, the man "took a great swallow and spread his arms and went into the air." I had to re-read that sentence again to understand what I thought it meant, almost taking my breath away.

After reading the article, I thought back to my New York theatrical agency days. One instance took me to the CBS television studios in mid-Manhattan.

As I left those studios to return to my office, Jimmy Breslin and a couple of other people were leaving for the same area I was going, so we all shared a taxi. While in that cab, I told Breslin how my Utica friend used to rave about him in college.

When we all got out of the cab, Jimmy said to me, "Where do you hang out"?

I told him Tweeds, the name of a bar/restaurant I frequented at the time. Jimmy asked if it wasn't named after William "Boss" Tweed, which was about all I knew about the name. He filled me in that Tweed was New York City's Public Works Commissioner in the late 1800's and was convicted and sent to jail for handing out bribes to win approval for a bond. When Breslin and I said our farewells, he didn't say he'd come to see me at Tweeds, but there was an inference that perhaps that was a possibility.

He, in fact, never did.

It was those thoughts I mused over in my wife's hospital room after having read Breslin's article of the guy who jumped off the Brooklyn Bridge.

By the way, it took 14 years to build the Brooklyn Bridge and 20 laborers lost their lives doing so, including the chief engineer, John Augustus Roebling. Oh … the limestone used in the bridge towers is from nearby Canajoharie.

In Jimmy Breslin's farewell *Newsday* newspaper column, dated Nov. 2, 2004, after 16 years there, his last line read: "Thanks for the use of the hall."

Breslin is a lifelong New Yorker and won the distinguished Pulitzer Prize for Commentary in 1986. He is the author of over a dozen books, among them, *"The Gang Who Couldn't Shoot Straight," "Forsaking All Others"* and *"World Without End, Amen."*

My friend from Utica, who used to talk about him so highly in our college days, pegged him well.

But most importantly, my wife's carpal tunnel surgery went smoothly.

Ever Been to Utica, Sammy?

April 12, 2006

A few weeks ago, my son Deane and I had dinner at a Syracuse restaurant.

As we were eating, I heard a Sammy Davis song on their sound system.

I then told Deane how, after Utica College, at the first job I had in New York City working in the mailroom of a big theatrical agency, one of my jobs was to deliver scripts and contracts to actors, producers, and directors. I made $65 a week and had to wear a suit.

One late morning, after I was out doing one of those tasks, I come back to the J.C. Penney building where our offices were located. The elevators were situated in such a way that there were banks of them, depending on the floor you were going to.

On that morning, I came to the aisle where any one of those elevators would take me to my floor and I noticed one of the doors was starting to close. I lunged for it and just made it in. As the doors closed, there I was looking at the only passenger in the elevator ... Sammy Davis, Jr.

It all happened so fast, all I could think to say was, "Sammy, what's happening?"

He said, "Everything's cool," and in the twelve or so seconds it took to get to his floor, he was intently staring at the front ceiling where all the floors told you where you were at that second. Observing what I perceived to be his private thoughts, which certainly didn't include me, I didn't force further conversation.

When the elevator got to the floor occupied by the film

producer Joseph E. Levine (*Godzilla*, *Hercules*, *The Graduate*), Sammy got off.

In the years since, from time to time, I've thought of what I could have said to him but obviously didn't:

- That I used to sing in the bathroom of the home in Utica I grew up in and for a time, while shaving, would play and sing over Sammy's unmistakable rendition of his hit song, "That Old Black Magic."
- And how I was knocked out by his acting in the film, *Anna Lucasta*," seeing him play the sailor to his romantic interest Eartha Kitt.
- And, that I saw that picture at the Lincoln Theatre my uncle owned in West Utica.

Would any of that have impressed Sammy? Probably not, but it couldn't have been worse than the only words I said to him, albeit the hip expression at the time, "What's happening?"

At that Syracuse restaurant, my son looked at me with silent interest when I told him, what I just imparted to you.

I didn't tell him that I didn't do a bad rendition of "That Old Black Magic."

Nothing like Sammy, of course.

But not bad.

A Killer? A Thief, Maybe...

July 5, 2006

It was 1969.

The acting class had just concluded and I was walking up the Greenwich Village, New York City street with the teacher Jack Manning and a couple of the other students. It was my first class with him at the H.B. Studios and, he had given all of us the task to perform a scene from a play of our choice for the next class.

As we all walked along, I asked Jack if he had any scene suggestions for me.

He questioned if I had ever read the play *Rashomon* that took place in Japan. After replying I hadn't, he told me about the lead character Tajomaru, a killer and thief who roamed the Japanese forests.

One of the qualities that attracted me to acting was the possibility of playing not only positive roles, but also roles you best not live in real life.

I purchased the play *Rashomon* and performed a scene from it in class, using two other classmates for the scene, an attractive female and her boyfriend who played the roles of husband and wife.

The scene took place deep within a Japanese forest. Tajomaru had overtaken the husband, a Japanese soldier, tied him up, and was circling the woman who had captured his fancy.

Tajomaru was so taken by her that he told her he'd do anything if she would be his woman, even going so far as to getting a job pulling a cart in the city. She rebuffed him and he snapped, threatening to kill her if she didn't submit to him.

Responding to his powerful and unrestrained strength, she questioned how she wouldn't consider such a thing with her husband still alive. Tajomaru looked at the husband, picked up a large stick and calmly stated that he'd end that problem by simply killing him. He approached the husband and while raising the stick – it was at that point while I was playing Tajomaru – I heard a gasp from some of the students observing the scene.

Recently, I was watching the *Turner Classic Movie* channel. The host, Robert Osborne, was interviewing the actress Mia Farrow. They discussed the next picture about to be shown, *Rashomon*.

Mia had a younger sister, Tisa Farrow. When I took Jack Manning's acting class, it was in winter. The following summer, Jack taught a six-week acting workshop in Paget, Bermuda. He invited me to take it, which I did. Seventeen aspiring actors participated in it, with Tisa one of them.

Toward the end of that acting workshop, Jack was interviewed on a local Bermuda television talk show. During that show, selected students from his workshop performed short scenes. One of the students from our acting class and I performed a scene from the Neil Simon play, *The Odd Couple*. I played the nitpicking Felix Unger.

Since our form of transportation around Bermuda was by mopeds, I drove around downtown Paget after that TV show – slowly – stopping frequently … hoping someone would say, "Didn't I see you on TV?" But alas, not a nibble.

What price, fame?

I recently looked up Jack Manning and Tisa Farrow on the internet. Both have enjoyed interesting film careers.

I never saw Tisa after those Bermuda acting days, but subsequently did see Jack in Los Angeles. In addition to teaching acting, Jack had an impressive resume as an actor and director.

After the New York acting phase of my life, I moved to Los Angeles, opening my own theatrical agency, *The Barry Damsky Agency*. I wanted to represent him as a client and he came to see me. He was his usual wonderful charming self, but representing him wasn't meant to be.

A lot of things weren't.

Viewing *Rashomon* at home recently was a riveting experience. What a superb movie!

Funny how events and people wend their way in and out of one's life.

But most importantly, on to the exciting and precious future!

You Want Me to Get – What?

September 19, 2007

A few Sundays ago on my birthday, we were having dinner in my kitchen with my wife, daughter, son and mother-in-law – all grooving on pizza and antipasto.

My daughter was telling us all about Boldt Castle in Alexandria Bay, New York, she had visited the previous day. My wife and children have been on the boat tour several times that takes you to Boldt Castle, letting off all those who want to visit it. For those choosing not to, the tour continues on. The next tour boat picks up those who were left off to see the castle.

On the occasions we've taken that tour, we haven't taken advantage of getting off and visiting the castle.

As my daughter described the castle, my wife and I listened with great interest. For instance, it has enough rooms for 25 families of four, is six stories high and has gorgeous grounds.

I asked, "Didn't the guy who had it built have it done for his girlfriend who died?"

My mother-in-law politely corrected me, explaining that when it was built many years ago by the owner of the Waldorf Astoria Hotel in New York City, it was as a token of his love for his wife. And, that before it was completed, she died, so he lost interest and construction was halted and never finished.

Those who visit Boldt Castle see that incompletion, as well as the beauty and expansiveness of what was completed.

It was in the mid '60s and I was working for the head of the television department at the Ashley-Famous theatrical agency in New York City.

One unforgetable day, my boss, Bobby Brenner, instructed me that our client Dinah Shore was recording that day and, I would be expected to be there with them.

I was new to the job and was star-struck that I'd see the famous Dinah Shore. And, since I had a particular love for music, seeing such a famous person in those types of surroundings, well – it was an exciting double whammy.

During the recording, I was in one of the outer rooms when – suddenly – I was summoned to where Bobby and Dinah were. I was told that Dinah had ripped the slacks she was wearing. I was given precise instructions to take a cab to the famous Waldorf Astoria Hotel where she was staying and to enter the building from the side street, whose entrance was called Waldorf Towers. She gave me the key to her suite, with instructions where to find "them".

Taking the side street elevators up to her suite, I was most impressed with its opulence. I went to a large bedroom where – sure enough – a pair of white slacks lay on the bed. I then took them back to where she was recording, handing them to her as if they were the Hope Diamond. Dinah was so grateful and I thought it was a big deal that I had rescued her in that manner – for such an important person as she.

And that's the story I told my family three Sundays ago in my kitchen as we ate my birthday cake.

If the opportunity presents itself and we take that Boldt Castle boat tour, this time we'll get off and take the tour.

For the former owner of the Waldorf Astoria Hotel in New York who had it built, and for Dinah who stayed at his hotel – when I sort of rescued her, well … please allow me to defer to the expression, "The tie that binds."

Suh, Suh, Suh, Sal, Is That Really You?

May 21, 2008

The headline in the April 28, 2008 Utica *Observer-Dispatch* poked at me.

It read, "Ex-convicts stage play."

The article was about a play that recently opened in New York about four ex-convicts who act out their respective true - life stories: one, who was arrested 67 times, and another, who killed a man when 17, spending 30 years in jail.

The four actors are members of an organization founded by theatrical agent and producer David Rothenberg. That organization helps ex-convicts rejoin the world. It went on to say that David Rothenberg produced the play *Fortune and Men's Eyes* in the late '60s.

That definitely got me.

In the late '60s, while living in New York attempting to be a working actor, I read about that *Fortune and Men's Eyes* audition in one of the show business trade papers.

I had gone to acting school the previous year.

I was cleaning a bar seven days a week. I also had my Utica high school skill of being able to type, supplementing my income with any number of temporary employment agencies who offered me jobs doing that.

With that lifestyle, I was able to take acting auditions as they came up.

Mentioned in that long ago *Fortune and Men's Eyes* audition in the show business trade paper, was the director, Sal Mineo. I had seen Sal, along with James Dean in the classic movie *Rebel Without a Cause*, at the elegant Stanley Theatre in Utica. Sal was nominated for Best Supporting Actor for that film.

When I arrived at the theatre where the audition for *Fortune and Men's Eyes* took place, it wasn't long before my number was called.

I walked down the long aisle of that dark theatre and was instructed by the man who sat on the lip of the stage, to sit in the first seat in the first row.

After sitting down and looking up at him, only then did I realize it was Sal Mineo. It was just him and me. I could hardly believe it.

The James Dean film Sal was in was about the general rebellion of youth I so related to and had such an effect on me, that seeing Sal one-on-one like that, well – it was as if I were in another world. Here I was actually talking to a famous actor like him to begin with, and more importantly, talking with someone who had personally known the great James Dean!

Sal asked me my background. I told him I was doing the menial jobs to be able to take auditions such as his.

I then got brave and asked him what James Dean was really like.

In a sincere and easy-going manner, Sal explained how James was an unusually sensitive human being who, in the time he had known him, was a true friend.

I didn't get the part Sal was looking for.

But I never forgot meeting him, a friend of James Dean, one of the greatest acting legends of the twentieth century … whose tragic death at the age of 24 included just three film masterpieces, *Rebel Without a Cause*, *East of Eden* and *Giant*.

Sal went on to direct and star in the play, *Fortune and Men's*

Eyes in New York and Los Angeles.

I never earned a paying acting role.

I was cast in an off-off Broadway, non-paying original play in the East Village of New York. I was subsequently cast for a non-paying acting role in a comedic play for a prestigious New York theatre organization I was most excited about, figuring my break had finally come. It wasn't long after that, they called and told me they were abandoning the play.

But I'd like to think I grew as a human being from that entire acting effort such as it was; that included the rejection I had come to know only too well.

They say, "No pain, no gain."

Hopefully so.

Acting photograph I never used, 1969

Life on 72nd Street

December 17, 2008

The first memory I have of New York City was in a taxi with my dad. We were on our way from the train station to our hotel in mid-Manhattan. I must have been about eight.

Having been brought up in Utica, small compared to New York, just looking out from that taxi, I had never seen so many people, so much traffic, so many neon signs and such wondrously tall buildings. And the noise – all of it was rather incredible. Probably still is. But above and beyond experiencing that entire "jaw-dropping" new world, there was an electricity about it all ... that unmistakable energy that is unique to New York City.

Working my first job there after college, I vividly remember the first time I visited West 72nd Street, specifically the one-block area between Broadway and West End Avenue. There was something about it I had not experienced in any other part of New York. I eventually ended up living on that very exciting block for five years.

It had everything – a bank, a famous delicatessen, a fabulous fancy take-out food store and two bars, one of which I worked at for a good part of the five years I lived in that neighborhood. On each side of my small apartment building were two stores: one, a most interesting gift shop where they had the most clever holiday cards I've ever seen before or since; the second, a small corner grocery store where I was introduced when in season, to the superb world of Casaba melons.

In the summer, I would ascend the couple of floors to the roof of my apartment building, and from there, could observe the constant ebb and flow of life on West 72ⁿᵈ Street below.

I would walk the short distance to the nearby end of 72ⁿᵈ Street where it merged with the West Side Highway. Adjoining that area, was a beautiful jogging track I took advantage of. I would also go to that area just for its peaceful and soothing demeanor.

I also discovered a glorious elevated, private location just to the side of where traffic entered and exited that West Side Highway, where I could observe below the freight trains coming in and out of the city. From there, I could also see the short distance across the Hudson River to New Jersey.

And there was the view looking at the New York side, where impressive, high-rise buildings loomed as far as the eye could see. Just observing the vehicles coming from the West Side Highway had a high intensity rhythm. And from that totally private spot – while looking across the river – I once sang my heart out.

But above all, New York's energy was always evident and continues to be. When you think of it – stuffing an international populous of millions into a finite island – well, that's what you get … a classic melting pot of concentrated humanity.

Those were turbulent, passionate, life-chasing years full of dreams that advanced me, in part, to where I am now. Of course, wherever you are, life contributes to that. But I especially remember those long ago New York City days.

At the end of West 72nd St. in New York City
seeking peace and tranquility, 1970

He Was All in Black

October 14, 2009

Earlier in the year, I was at a store in Utica. While there, playing on the store's music system was Neil Diamond's song, "Sweet Caroline."

When I heard it, I thought of Neil's influence in my life, particularly since the drummer on "Sweet Caroline" – Gene Crisman – was the drummer when I recorded two songs in Nashville seven years ago.

I met Neil, a client of the theatrical agency I worked for, years earlier in New York. I placed him on a local New York musical television show. He was just beginning his career. At that show, in my communication with him, he was very quiet, and although polite, didn't have any concerns that required my assistance. He knew I was around if he needed me. That's how it works with talent and agents at shows like that.

Years later, when living in Los Angeles, I attended one of the earliest showings of the movie that Neil starred in, *The Jazz Singer*. One of the executives I had worked with years earlier at the New York theatrical agency, had since left the agency and was the producer of that film. He was greeting those exiting the theatre and asking their responses to the movie. Seeing him brought back memories of my earlier New York theatrical agency days.

Because I was struggling to improve my singing career and just having seen Neil's character in the film going through his struggles to make it as a successful singer ... well – let's just say – it all got to me.

So those were some of the jumbled thoughts I had as I listened to Neil's song at that Utica store.

Speaking of music, my wife and I recently saw the Levon Helm Band at the Stanley Theatre in Utica.

A singer, drummer and mandolin player, Levon played with Conway Twitty, Bob Dylan, and among others, the famous group, The Band. In 1996, Levon developed throat cancer, but at that time, had beat it. One of Levon's big hits with his band performing it at the Stanley – just before his encore – was "The Weight."

When the Utica local radio announcer introduced Levon and his group, he told us all there that Levon would be playing the drums, but due to a nodule on Levin's throat being removed recently, would not be singing. And, throughout the entire concert where Levon mostly played the drums and frequently the mandolin, he spoke not a word.

Levon came out to a raucous, appreciative crowd and he and his incredible world-class musicians played a concert that was one of the best I've ever experienced.

When the concert concluded, as Levon was about to leave the stage, he gestured to the audience with his hands clasped together, bowing to the crowd in sincere appreciation. Knowing his throat cancer background, it was a stirring moment.

Do me a favor, if Levon Helm performs anywhere near where you are, run – don't walk – to see him.

Oh, and the next time you hear "Sweet Caroline," zone in on the drummer.

(Since the above column was published, Levon Helm passed away from his battle with cancer.)

Rod – Wow – So Pleased to Meet You!

October 28, 2009

There was a considerable newspaper article in the Sept. 30 Utica *Observer-Dispatch* about Rod Serling's highly successful TV series which he wrote and hosted, *Twilight Zone*. The original show ran from 1959-1964.

The show's 50th anniversary was recently celebrated in Binghamton, New York, where Serling grew up. He attended Binghamton Central High School where, in front of that school, a historical marker stands informing all who read it that Rod went there.

Rod's *Twilight Zone* show has been the subject of many books, magazines, comic books, a radio series, a Steven Spielberg film, and more recently, blogs and web sites. It's reported that the show will appear in a future film from Leonardo DiCaprio's production company. The show also has had continued popularity through television syndication in DVD form and is under license to air in 30 countries.

And all because of Rod Serling.

I was standing in the long hallway of the New York theatrical agency. It was after most of the activity of the day was completed and my boss and I were two of the few who were still there. I saw my boss and someone coming toward me and was then introduced to that person, Rod Serling.

My boss disappeared momentarily into his office and Rod and I were left to talk to each other. I was thrilled to be in such a famous man's presence, particularly in a one-on-one situation. I knew he had contributed to writing a play that was on Broadway at that time, and remarked to him how he must be so excited for his latest accomplishment.

He enthusiastically responded how thrilled he was because of that. Knowing how much this man had done in his life and his joy for that accomplishment was so evident in his response to me, I found myself feeling proud for him, even though I really didn't personally know him.

My boss shortly came out of his office with big bags of bread and sandwiches he had bought at the nearby famous Stage Deli, where so many show business people ate. Rod lived in Ithaca and my boss and he were about to travel there, replete with all the great Stage Deli goodies.

Over the years, I've met – albeit on a cursory level – many show business personalities and performers. Recalling Rod's meeting, I reflect on what a sincere and warm personality he had for the brief time we communicated.

That's not always the case, at least in my experience. You're going to have to trust me on this one because I can't tell you his name. One time, I was with another television agent of our firm, along with a big time comedian we represented.

Suddenly, the comedian started yelling and questioning what kind of agency he was represented by with an agent like me who wasn't clean shaven, which was true. In limpid defense – although I didn't dare mention it to him – growing beards and mustaches were in vogue at the time.

But when he exploded and criticized me, in the rather brutal manner he did, I felt like disappearing anyplace that would take me, whether a crack in the sidewalk or some dark cellar somewhere.

But you take the bad with the good – good being the positive experience I had with Rod Serling and the not so good with the comedian who didn't care for my facial experimentation.

Go figure.

He Was Very Low-Keyed

September 15, 2010

I had watched the Syracuse/Akron college football game on TV a couple of Saturdays ago, most pleased that Syracuse beat them handily, particularly since Syracuse has had such a bleak football record for the past number of years. After the game, I switched to one of the movie channels and found the film *The Graduate* playing.

When I was a New York theatrical agent, the firm had a meeting every week with all us agents sitting around a large conference table. Each agent would report his individual progress in acquiring employment for clients for whichever department we represented; in my case, it was television. It was standard procedure and that was how all the agents knew what was going on in the firm, particularly the executives who didn't attend the meetings, reading the minutes later.

For two of the three years I was there, when it came her turn, the head of the Motion Picture Department would enthusiastically report about a particular new actor she had signed to the firm and at each weekly meeting predicted how that actor would be a big star. After a while, we all accepted her glowing activity for him as normal.

She excitedly told us at one meeting of him getting a big break with a starring role in a major film. We all looked up at that one.

Then it happened on one monumental meeting day.

When it came her turn to summarize what her department had done that past week, she sat there and said in an exhaustive and peaceful way, she had seen her actor's private film screening the previous evening that would make her actor a superstar. At that point, I knew something important had happened and that I was witness to some kind of theatrical agency film history.

The film she had seen in that private screening the previous night was, *The Graduate*.

Her actor - Dustin Hoffman.

About six months after the film came out, with the public accepting Dustin in the successful manner it did, I was walking up New York's 5th Avenue with a fellow agent/friend of our agency. Walking alone toward us was Dustin.

My agent/friend had met him through our firm and as I hadn't, he introduced us. We stood there making small talk. I congratulated him on his success in *The Graduate*, further asking him if he was enjoying that success. He was polite, soft spoken and appeared to appreciate what I had said, glowingly affirming that success. The next time I saw him was a couple of years later after I had left the agency business … in *The Graduate*. As expected, it was exciting seeing him in it then, as well as at my home recently.

I've reflected on those "glamour" years, and from time to time have been asked if they were exciting. My response has been, and still is, they were.

But then again, glamour or not, isn't all of life - exciting?

Los Angeles

Second Fiddle to Hot Chocolate

May 2, 2007

I recently read about "speed-dating", a new way of meeting the possible significant love of your life. It took place at a Hollywood, Florida, night club. You met your perspective date for seven minutes, sitting on a chair facing each other, and then moved to the next chair clockwise for another round of the same, seeing seven candidates in that fashion.

A bunch of blind dates, each for seven minutes.

Got me to thinking …

It was in the late '70s and I was living in Los Angeles.

Unbeknownst to me, one of my friends submitted my name to the then popular television show, *The Dating Game* hosted by Jim Lange. If you were on the show, you were one of three contestants competing for a date with the opposite sex.

The show called me asking if I'd be interested in trying out for it.

Since my romantic life was stuck on zero, I said, "Yes." I auditioned for it and was called several days later and told I made the show; at the same time, I was given a taping date.

The taping of the show took place at a theatre/studio in Hollywood.

They rehearsed you all day so you'd know what to expect, not telling you what to say, but in great detail, explaining how the show would proceed. The reason it took all day to do that was because they were taping a number of shows, one after another, and they'd explain to you one facet of the show, and you'd wait around until they did the same for the others who would be involved in those other shows.

And sure enough, the show I appeared on was taped with a live audience.

Of the three guys trying to win our show's date, one was a medical doctor, the other a body guard for the famous singer Alice Cooper, and I was introduced as, "an administrative assistant at UCLA and a great singer." The reason I use these exact words is because I have the video tape of the show and am quoting Jim Lange precisely.

The game went by quickly. My only recollection of it being it was a larger audience than I had anticipated.

And then it came time for the girl to decide her date.

She chose me.

Back stage, she and I sat together for a couple of minutes, and as we talked briefly … she told me she loved skiing.

I had won not only a chauffer-driven date with her, but also dinner at a Hollywood restaurant, along with tickets to a play at the Huntington Hartford Theatre in Los Angeles.

When several weeks went by and I hadn't heard from the show, I called them.

They asked when I'd like to go out on the date. I told them any Saturday night.

I was called back and told the date was a ski enthusiast and that she didn't want to give up her Saturday night for the date, but during the week was fine. I told the show I'd think on that.

I then concluded that if the girl didn't want to make the sacrifice to give up her Saturday night preferring her skiing to our date, it was the tip of the "negative chemistry" iceberg between us – sensing a bad experience when I saw it. *Dating Game* or no *Dating Game*, I figured I didn't need the aggravation.

Sue me.

So I didn't call the show back and obviously never went on

the date.

When I tell the story from time to time about how I won the date on *The Dating Game*, invariably, I'm asked how the date went.

In fact, thinking about it and particularly if I watch the video of the show every once in a great while, it makes me smile.

Perhaps the show should have been called, "The Dating Game – Maybe."

It's Really Him! Heart Don't Fail Me!

July 16, 2008

I was talking on the phone to a sales representative from a Syracuse television station recently. Besides our usual advertising agency business, I always talk sports with him.

At the time, the Boston Celtics had just played the Lakers in Los Angeles in an NBA Playoffs game. I had seen a snippet of the game on TV and asked him if the usual personalities were there, mentioning Jack Nicholson and the film director Spike Lee.

He told me the TV cameras pointed them out as they usually do. He then asked me if I had heard of the rift between Spike Lee and Clint Eastwood, which I hadn't. He then explained they were having a disagreement about criticism Spike made of a couple of Clint's war films with the upshot that Clint gave his side of the argument ending with the suggestion to Spike that he,"shut his face" (*New York Daily News* 2008).

My Syracuse TV guy questioned why anyone would pick a fight with Clint Eastwood. I didn't argue his point.

I then told him that in the '70s I had my own theatrical agency in Los Angeles, representing talent. And that an actor I didn't know called me and told me he was in Clint's latest film at the time, *Magnum Force*.

That actor invited me to a private screening of that film because he didn't have an agent. He said that Clint was interested in him for a part in his next film as well. The understanding was that the actor and I would meet at the end of the screening of *Magnum*

Force, and if I liked what he did in the film, he'd give me Clint's phone number. I'd then call Clint, and if he wanted the actor in his next film, I'd negotiate the deal.

I went to the screening and met the actor whose performance in *Magnum Force* was small but respectable. He gave me Clint's phone number and we agreed I'd then call Clint to see if there was any further interest.

I called the number he gave me and left word on the answering machine, not quite sure if it was Clint's or not.

Days went by and it just happened that I had made arrangements to move into new offices for my agency. That alone was quite exciting, and as I walked into that suite of offices that first day – carrying my brief case in one hand and a small typewriter in the other – the shared office receptionist told me that Clint Eastwood was on the phone for me.

Excitedly entering my office, I picked up the phone and sure enough, I heard that familiar, unmistakable famous voice. It then hit me … I was on the phone with Clint Eastwood!

I told him about seeing the actor in *Magnum Force* at the screening and how that actor was under the impression Clint wanted him for his next film. And, if so, I'd negotiate the deal.

Clint patiently told me in his slow, western cadence that the actor was in fact in his film *Magnum Force* and that he had done a very nice job. He further stated he wasn't committed to not using him in his next film, but that it appeared unlikely … that, if he did, he'd contact me.

The recent reviews for *Magnum Force* were tremendous. I asked Clint – because of that – if he wasn't, in fact, most happy with the way life was going for him. In a sincere and humbling way, he responded that, yes, all of that was true and that he was in fact most pleased with how it was all going.

After finishing telling that story on the phone to my TV guy in

Syracuse, he then said, "You should write a book."

I told him that he was the third person as of late to have made that suggestion.

Maybe I should put that on my "To Do" list.

But you've got to admit, you just don't – write a book.

Do you?

What You've Got to Go Through

July 30, 2008

It was in the late '70s. I was living in Los Angeles.

I found myself at a job on Hollywood Boulevard. The purpose was to sit at a phone all day long and call engineers from a list I was given. I was to tell them that I represented an aircraft business (like Lockheed, which had engaged the firm to do that) and was setting up appointments for an engineering job that paid so much an hour. The more engineers I could get to go to those appointments, the more money I'd make.

My superior, whose task was the same as mine and about six others, continually beat us all. That's probably why he was our boss. One day I signed up 11 and tied him. His demeanor turned to distrust and scorn. Guess I threatened him, at least for that one day.

I became so discouraged with most of the engineers telling me "no", my subsequent low rate of success became obvious, and I was fired at the end of the week – which seemed to have lasted about 147 years.

But the saving grace of that job was that, on my lunch hour, I'd go across the street to a large antiquated building I was told was slated for demolition. There were a number of pianos in their many high-ceiling rooms. I introduced myself to the person in charge, explaining I was an aspiring singer and musician and requested if I could use one of their piano rooms during my lunch breaks.

I was told the pianos were in use most of the time on a first come, first serve basis, but if I found a room no one was in, I had the approval to use it.

I usually found one room empty that had the worst piano of them all, but I was grateful for the opportunity. For the brief time of those long ago lunch hours, I found solace playing and singing. The best piano of the lot had a small stage in the room, usually occupied by a middle-aged, male music writer. One of the days of that week, I got to that room before him, elated for the opportunity to play on what was an extraordinary grand piano. Midway through that practice, the music writer came in, most annoyed I was in "his room" even though those weren't the rules. He criticized me for attempting to enter the area of singing, which he declared only the most serious and talented prevailed, and how could I possibly think I'd ever enter that hallowed ground? And that the true test of a singer's worth was singing with no musical accompaniment – a cappella – and did I have the guts to stand up on the stage in that room, to show him I had that rare gift of talent that no way could I have.

I got up on the stage and sang a country song of haunting lonely love, and when finished, he was noticeably changed. He reluctantly and begrudgingly told me I had talent. What I then did I'm not proud of. I emotionally told him how egotistical he was, that I wasn't the fool he thought me to be, and that I had no respect for a condescending person such as he.

And walked out.

I don't know why I think of that long ago event, but I'm happy to say I somehow persevered, and in about two weeks, a CD of my gospel songs, "We Declare", is about to be released.

Hopefully, this perseverance business will finally come through for me.

You can only hope.

Don't Hover Over a Pool in a Helicopter

December 3, 2008

My wife and I were watching the Kris Kristofferson/Barbra Streisand film *A Star Is Born* on TV recently. As it progressed, I mentioned to her that when I had my LA theatrical agency, I was instrumental in placing one of the actors I represented, Machine Gun (M.G.) Kelly, in that film. M.G. was Los Angeles's #1 radio disc jockey.

I was instrumental in getting him two roles: the first, playing a big city radio disc jockey in *A Star Is Born*, obviously not a stretch in character. If you see the rerun of it, you'll see his role required acting ability, as he has a tumultuous relationship with Kris Kristofferson's character, John Norman Howard.

On a day Kelly wasn't shooting, he invited me to the set at Warner Brothers. Kristofferson and Streisand were the only other actors there, and M.G. and I kept a safe distance from them. About a half hour went by when Kelly was called away for a few moments, returning to inform me that, because it was a closed set, we'd have to leave.

In one of the scenes in the film, Kristofferson's character, John Norman, walks into the radio station Kelly's character, Bebe Jesus, was broadcasting from. John Norman was carrying a case of booze as a peace offering. He had taken a pistol shot at Bebe the previous day when Bebe was in a helicopter hovering over John Norman's pool trying to get an on-air story from him. John Norman didn't like his personal space being invaded and took a pistol shot at Bebe to drive him away, which did the trick.

That next day, John Norman tells Bebe he was sorry for what he had done. Bebe grabs his radio microphone and goes on the air telling his listeners that John Norman's there and spews venom at John Norman who can't take Bebe's taunting – to the degree John hurls the case of booze through the broadcasting booth window where Bebe was broadcasting from. The impact of flying glass forces Bebe back off his chair landing on the back wall. When you see the film, you'll understand how, after shooting that scene, Kelly told me, for a few days, he had a sore back.

Coincidentally, the next film that came on, after watching *A Star Is Born* with my wife at home, was Clint Eastwood's *The Enforcer*. I was instrumental in getting Kelly a role playing a priest in that film.

As the film progressed, Clint was chasing one of the bad guys who ran into Kelly's church with Eastwood in hot pursuit. Kelly then gets mad at Eastwood for barging into his "hallowed" church. It broke the mold of Kelly playing just a disc jockey. It was a good scene and watching it with my wife brought back memories.

Kelly called me about six years ago here in Boonville and when I got on the phone, the first thing I heard was him giving the venomous speech he gave to Kristofferson's character in *A Star Is Born*. Kelly now lives in Las Vegas, is married and has a child. He's still very much involved with show business. This past year, he emailed me to visit him in Las Vegas.

Maybe.

The Palomino

May 13, 2009

When my daughter was preparing for her recent trip out west, knowing a part of her trip would be in Los Angeles, it stirred up a lot of old memories when I lived there in the 70's.

At one point, to survive, I used an old talent I had from my high school days in Utica – typing. Life handed me that gift in the form of being able to type accurately and fast. So I typed for the highest employer bidder and that's how I paid my bills.

I found myself typing exclusively for the UCLA employment agency for various departments. Wherever they placed me, I was always in close proximity to UCLA's music school, taking advantage by using any of their many piano rooms. If there was a piano room available, its door would be open. Most of the time, I'd find one and to the accompaniment of the piano, I'd work out my voice, at that time, singing country music.

I heard about the Palomino, the country and western club in Los Angeles that featured all the big names in country music. Thursdays were their open talent night. I'd go there at 6 p.m. on any Thursday and the first 50 would sign in. Now, the music didn't start until eight p.m. so you'd hang around. When it started, you never knew what time the emcee would call your name to perform your one song. At the end of the evening, someone won the competition.

I went there and sang on and off for the last five years I lived in LA. My best effort was the first time I performed there, singing the James Taylor song, *Bartender Blues*, about a bartender who's not happy with his job. I was drawn to the song's theme, for I was a part-time New York City bartender back in my acting days, when I lived there prior to Los Angeles.

The Palomino's house band was superb, receiving country awards for years for "Best Backup Band".

In one instance, I sang late in the evening with just an acoustic guitar. It was a country ballad and at that time of the night, not many there were interested in the low-keyed song I sang, albeit, about lost love country conveys so well.

I received a light smattering response and went back to where I was sitting. Next to me sat a couple; the man I can only describe as a rough-looking, bearded country type who wore a cowboy hat he could have been a model for.

I saw a hand coming toward me out of the corner of my eye as he said, "I enjoyed your song very much - very much."

He had a heavy presence about him and when he said it, I believed him. I was so ecstatic at least one person enjoyed it, particularly since he seemed so authentic and imposing.

The Palomino is no longer there. One of the two owner brothers died and the club couldn't afford the high prices the big acts demanded

I no longer sing country; instead, I'm immersed in spiritual music, particularly gospel.

Recently, at home, I came across a long-sleeved pullover Palomino shirt I've never worn I suspect is a collector's item.

Oh … Bob Dylan and Jerry Lee Lewis, among others, sang there.

Not on a Thursday night.

Me at the Palomino one Thursday night. The *Los Angeles Times* (12/11/71) called it, "Country music's most important west coast club."

I Auditioned on That Stage

May 27, 2009

I'm a dreamer. Always have been. I wouldn't have attempted vocations like acting and singing if I wasn't.

When living in Los Angeles in the '70s, I heard that the Stanley Theatre in Utica was seeking a theatre manager. With my background in the theatrical agency business in New York and in Los Angeles, the position seemed realistic.

So I wrote my Aunt Pearl Nathan in Utica, stating my interest in the position and filling her in on my background. The reason I wrote her was because she was very involved with the Stanley. When it went through hard times and was being threatened by the wrecking ball, she saved the theatre by organizing and raising funds for it from the local arts and business community.

She wrote back responding I was being considered for the Stanley position.

Since I was involved in singing country music at that time, I had an idea for a TV show I'd produce and host that I would offer to whichever Utica television station would run it. The show would have featured local country talent on their way up, along with established talent performing in the general geographical area as they passed through. I was close to that type of production as a television agent in New York City, so it wasn't that unrealistic.

Six months prior to leaving LA to return back east to Utica, I had been attending a television newscasting school, the result of which was that I had a video tape of me delivering a newscast.

So, armed with the Stanley Theatre manager possibility, the TV country show idea and my TV news tape, I returned to my home roots of Utica with great hope in my heart.

I didn't get the Stanley position and I wasn't able to get the country TV show off the ground, although I sure tried. One of the two Utica television stations taped me for an audition for on-air news, but none of it was meant to be.

The closest I got to the Stanley Theatre situation was winning an audition held there for the role as the emcee of a live magic show produced by a gentleman who owned a lion. They both lived in the Utica suburb of New York Mills. One rehearsal night, several weeks prior to the show, I was told by the producer, that he was going to replace me as the emcee.

Which he did.

Recently, for our 26th wedding anniversary, our children treated my wife and me to a night at the Stanley to see Michael Flatley's great Irish singing and dancing production, "Lord of the Dance."

As I sat there, I thought how the Stanley had played the role it had in my life. And all the memories I had of it from watching films there as I grew up, among them, *Rebel Without a Cause*, and seeing live shows there the likes of Bob Dylan and Dolly Parton, and how that incredible theater, one of the finest in the world to this day, had fed my dreams.

And quite honestly, still does.

Ah dreams.

May there always be dreamers.

A Singing Newscaster?

September 1, 2010

I was at my Utica optometrist's office recently and found myself telling her about my Los Angeles UCLA typing days. I would take more of a break than I should have in the mid-mornings and played and sang in their piano rooms at their music school, mostly on their upright pianos. Of the many piano rooms, two had grand pianos. If a door were open to any of those piano rooms, I would quietly slip into the first one I could find. If I found more than one door open, I would try out each piano and take the best one.

One UCLA late piano room afternoon, I was fortunate enough to find the best grand piano room door open. It was the only time it happened, and I was ecstatic being able to work out on such a fine piano.

I was attending a television news broadcasting school in Hollywood five nights a week. We'd have a lecture for an hour and then our class would produce a 30-minute newscast. When at the end after taping it, the show was played back and we were all critiqued for whatever our contribution was. One student's assignment was to produce it, another to direct, two camera people, a news anchor, a co-anchor, one to do sports, one for the weather and a couple to work the video machines. I tried mostly to get the anchor or co-anchor opportunities as much as I could, thinking at that moment of my life, I'd be a TV newscaster somewhere.

When the anchor or co-anchor spots were taken, I would volunteer for the weather spot no one cared for. I'd have fun with it, attempting to aim my deliveries in a comedic style.

During the seven or so months I faithfully attended that TV

news school, we students were all given the opportunity to do a special project. I chose to produce, with our class, a half-hour variety show I hosted and performed in. I still have the video tape of it. Every once in a great while, I'll watch it. There's a part in that show where I sing and dance to a country song, "Rusty Old Halo." It's about people who don't always do the right thing in life and just barely make it to heaven. I'm dressed as an angel, replete with halo, wearing "a robe that's so wooly that it scratches." It's pretty funny.

I went to a Hollywood music store and rented a grand piano for that show. I was told it was the piano that the song, "The Entertainer," was recorded on. That song, written by Scott Joplin and arranged by Marvin Hamlisch, was made famous in the movie *The Sting*. Because I used that piano for that long ago project, you could say, I was famous - by proxy.

In that 30-minute show, among other things, I sang and accompanied myself on the piano to the song, "C'est La Vie." When I was practicing it at UCLA at that grand piano that one time, in the middle of it, the door opened, and a young music student with a violin quietly slipped in, and without a word, accompanied me on his violin. When he soloed at the instrumental part of the song, he was extraordinary; it was a moment in life I'll always remember. When the song was over, he silently left as quietly as he had arrived.

I never saw him again.

That's the story I told my optometrist.

Don Martin School of Broadcasting, Hollywood, California.
Me singing for a taped school newscast. (I was supposed to be a
budding singer). The guitar was borrowed from a student from
Mexico who requested I marry her so she could get her Green
Card. I told her when I married, it would be for love. 1980

Crime, Ah, Doesn't Pay

October 5, 2011

I heard recently from my cousin Ellen who lives in Boston. Her grandfather and my father were brothers. In the '70s, when I lived in Los Angeles, she came there to visit her friends.

I was living in a boarding house in mid Los Angeles run by an eccentric elderly woman who had a grand piano. She went away one weekend, was mad at me for a reason I have conveniently blocked, and, as punishment, before she left, locked the piano. That weekend I broke the lock to it and sang and played on it.

With great trepidation, I awaited her return, knowing "my goose" was more than amply cooked.

When she came back and discovered the unwanted physical intrusion to her piano, she – sometime later and rightly so – kicked me out. Luckily, she didn't have me arrested.

I subsequently rented a room in a beautiful house in Beverly Hills. That home also had a grand piano. One "adult-beveraged" two a.m. Sunday morning – thinking she was away for the weekend – I sang and heartily played on it, only to find out later that day that – surprisingly – she was there all the time. She never said anything about it, nor might I add, did I.

When my cousin Ellen came to visit, I picked her up at LA's cavernous train station located in the downtown area.

LA's laws against jaywalking are simple – it's against the law.

I parked my car in the lot opposite the train station. Walking toward the street that separated that parking lot from the station, I stood directly opposite its entrance.

It was a very hot day.

The closest marked-off area for crossing the street was about 50 feet to the right of where I was standing. To get to it would have taken me an extra 20 seconds. Scanning traffic in both directions, I took a chance that "the law" wasn't around to see me … and, I started jaywalking toward the train station entrance. Reaching the middle of the street, I glanced to my right and there – not 30 yards from me in traffic coming toward me – was a police car.

My heart started beating strangely – more like pounding – a lot.

What flashed through my mind was to stop right there – in the middle of the street – and turn to the police car, hold up both arms and … surrender.

Did I do "dat"?

Not exactly.

Instead, I continued swiftly – more like jogged – through the entrance to the train station thinking I'd vanish among those there.

When inside, I disappeared into the crowd, figuring the inhabitants of that police car gave up on me, if they were interested in me at all.

About 30 seconds later – figuring I was safe – I turned around to head toward where I thought the entrances to the trains were. There, suddenly looking down at me, was a police officer, who politely handed me a ticket for jaywalking.

I received an email from my cousin Ellen recently, and in it, she referred to that long ago jaywalking incident.

When I went to the LA police station to pay the fine, the woman at the window treated me as if I was a fugitive.

For about 30 seconds, I was.

She should have only known what I did to the boarding house lady's piano.

Danny

January 4, 2012

Somebody recently mentioned Danny Thomas's name. I then told that person that I had met Danny in the mid 70s when I had my own theatrical agency in Los Angeles.

I represented a client whose background was as a professional baseball announcer. I was instrumental in getting him a job as the host of a Los Angeles sports-talk radio show.

That client convinced me he had the talent to "warm-up" live audiences, having done so when he lived in the Minneapolis area. A warm-up person talks to the live audience before the show and during lulls. His goal is to make the audience feel welcome and keep the audience's energy at an acceptable level.

I contacted the Danny Thomas organization, and my client and I were invited to a TV show Danny's production company was videotaping. When there, we were introduced to Danny Thomas. He was as warm and sincere in person, as his legions of fans knew him to be from the character he played in his successful television series, *Make Room for Daddy*. I told Danny I was from Utica, New York, and that my father, a normally quiet man, was a loyal, vocal fan of his. Danny was so sincerely appreciative of that. The man was genuine.

I looked Danny up on the internet.

Born Amos Muzyad Yakhoob Kairouz, he changed his name to Amos Jacobs, and then at his agent's request, to Danny Thomas.

As a struggling young entertainer at a time when his wife was pregnant – while at a Detroit church – Danny was so moved during the Mass, he put his last $7 in the collection box. The next day,

he landed a small acting part that paid 10 times his church dona-
tion the previous day.

Two years later, praying to St. Jude Thaddeus, the patron saint
of hopeless causes, Danny asked the saint, "Help me find my way
in life and I will build you a shrine."

He subsequently was successful and became internationally
known through films and television.

The title of his successful TV series, was suggested by his
wife, Rose Marie. Because of Danny's frequent show business
tours away from his family, she allowed the children to sleep with
her. When Danny would return, the children would empty dresser
drawers and leave the master bedroom to "make room for daddy."

True to his word, in 1955, Danny's shrine idea became a
reality for a children's hospital, St. Jude's Children's Research
Hospital in Memphis, Tennessee. Because of Danny's efforts, a
hospital was created devoted to curing children's catastrophic dis-
eases, as well as a research center for children of the world – all at
no cost to the patients.

Thomas developed a bedside manner. In observing a child crying, whose blood was being drawn from the youth's arm, Danny
requested a blood test for himself. In doing so, Danny cried, saying to the boy, "See, I cry, too." As the story goes, the little boy
smiled.

Marlo Thomas, Danny's daughter, quoted Danny: "There are
two kinds of people in the world, givers and takers. The takers
may eat better, but the givers sleep better."

So Danny's dream, of saving children's lives through St. Jude,
came true.

What a grand man. I'll take it one step further, what a great
man.

**A Hollywood agent. The Barry Damsky Agency.
Los Angeles, 1974.**

I Wanna Be in Pictures

June 13, 2012

On television recently, I saw the film *Funny Lady* with Barbra Streisand, James Caan and Omar Sharif.

It was 1973.

I had closed up my New York apartment and was back in Utica attempting to figure out my next life move. I had invested five years as an aspiring actor with nothing to show for it. The girl I was going with in New York, an aspiring actress, had moved to LA and wanted me to move there.

So I did.

Having been a theatrical agent with the big agency in New York, I knew all the agents of the firm in the New York and Los Angeles offices, and when I moved out to LA, I ran into a motion picture agent from that firm I knew from the years I worked for the agency.

He knew of my acting background, recommending I try out for the role of Billy Rose, the Broadway producer in the film *Funny Lady*. He thought I could play that role. He set it up and I went out to the Warner Bros. lot and interviewed with Jennifer Shull, the film's casting director.

So when I saw the film recently, it brought back memories of that experience.

As I watched the film at home, with James Caan playing the role, I questioned if I could have played that role with the life strength to romantically play opposite Barbra Streisand, notwithstanding what it would take to play Billy's life as a Broadway producer.

James Caan, who landed the role I auditioned for, played it

I WANNA BE IN PICTURES

to perfection.

I just read that actors are basically insecure people playing roles they couldn't pull off in real life, and that may or may not be so. Were I to have had an opportunity to have played that role in the film, would my imagination and acting talent have given me the strength to play it as I couldn't have truly played it in real life?

We'll never know.

When I shortly thereafter opened my own theatrical agency in LA, I represented an actress, Ildiko Jaid. She was divorced from John Drew Barrymore and emphasized that she couldn't take auditions at just any time, for she had a 2-year-old daughter she had to find a babysitter for.

Her 2-year-old daughter's name?

Drew Barrymore.

When I see Drew's work just about everywhere, I think of what might have been had I stayed in the LA theatrical agency business, knowing how she turned out.

Second guess questions of life. It's a fun but unrewarding game.

During my LA agency days, I was at a reception at Universal Studios with an actor I represented, Marco Lopez, who, at the time, was on the then popular television series, *Emergency*.

At that reception, we were talking to Mel Blanc, a wonderfully sincere man who was the voice of Bugs Bunny, Daffy Duck, Porky Pig, Tweety Bird, Sylvester the Cat, Yosemite Sam and others. Mel then did live – for Marco and me – the voice he created that the world knows as ...Woody Woodpecker.

What a privilege that was to hear him do that voice.

I laugh now thinking about it.

"Brushes" with the greats.

So far.

All for Sanity

June 27, 2012

As I was mowing the front lawn, a car stopped in front of our house and who should get out?

My long time friend, the old verbal flame-thrower himself – Casabubu.

I don't know what made me ask him, "What's wrong?" figuring whenever he goes out of his way to see me, something is up.

"Wrong?" he responded. "The only thing wrong is that humanity let you through its sanity doors!"

Attempting to restrain myself, I uttered, "You coming here, I thought maybe you needed my help in some small way."

"Bah-ree, the day I need your help is the day babies don't cry."

"All right," I told him. "So what's going on?"

"I got ah question about when you used to live in Los Angeles."

I knew something was up, responding with hesitation, "What would you like to know?"

"How did you get away from all the pressures that big city has?" he asked.

"Oh, that's easy," I told him. "From time to time, on weekends, I'd drive down to Mexico to get away from it all."

"Any one time worth mentioning?" he asked.

"Well," I stammered, "There was one time I drove to Rosarito Beach, Mexico, on Cinco de Mayo, one of Mexico's holidays, and found a motel on the ocean."

"So what's such ah big deal bow dat?"

"Funny you should ask."

I told him how I had driven to a nearby festival, celebrating that holiday with food, drink, general merriment and a mariachi band. When there, the mariachi band stopped at my table, where I was the only one sitting, and asked me what I wanted them to play. I quietly sang them a phrase I had remembered from the only Spanish song I knew."

"What was the phrase?" Casabubu asked.

I responded, "Cooka, cooka, coo ---."

"Did they know the song from that?" he asked.

"Yes," I proudly responded,

"You lucked out, you flop-head!" he said.

"Not really," I told him. "After they played the song, they asked me for another request, and since I didn't know any other Spanish songs, I suggested they choose one. After that song, they asked me for five dollars."

"Bah-ree, you're a colossal ding-dong! How could you have not known that would happen?"

I told him I wasn't the only one, for shortly after I paid them, an attractive young Mexican girl in a white dress came over to me, politely asking if I had to pay the band. When I told her I did, she told me the same thing occurred to her and her family.

"Then what happened?" Casabubu inquired.

I told him I asked the girl to dance, which we did, with her family all around me checking me out.

"You're lucky they didn't string you up on a tree," Casabubu commented, further inquiring, "And?"

"I asked her what her name was."

"Boy, I got to hand it to you Bah-ree, you ah feeble slickster. Did you get her phone number?"

"She told me she was from Chula Vista, California, but no, I didn't ask her for her phone number because everything happened so fast."

"Fast? In a race, you couldn't beat ah blind turtle!" Casabubu said.

I told him when I got back to Los Angeles, I looked up her name, Emma Torres, in the Chula Vista phone book.

"Did you find it?" he asked.

"She wasn't listed", I explained.

"So was that the end of it?" he pressed.

"Wait 'til you hear," I offered.

(To be continued in next column)

The Words and Music Just Came Pouring Out

July 11, 2012

In my last column, I was telling my friend, Casabubu, the story of when I lived in Los Angeles, and how, to escape the pressures of the city, I'd drive down to Mexico.

The first time I went down there to Rosarito Beach, I met a Spanish girl.

To be perfectly clear, the following happened five years before I met my wonderful wife.

When I returned to LA, I couldn't find the listing for the girl I met in Mexico in the Chula Vista, California, phone book.

"So, after you returned to LA and then couldn't track her down, was that the end of the story?" Casabubu asked.

I told him that I kept thinking about that girl, whose name was Emma Torres. Since I had no way of contacting her, I planned to return the next Cinco de Mayo holiday, where I met her the previous year at an outdoor festival. I hoped I had made the same impression on her as she had with me, and she'd be at the festival hoping I'd return.

"You're worse than a crazy dreamer," he said. "They should put you away. OK, I give up, was she there?"

"No," I responded.

"You crazy fool. How could you think she'd be there the next year?"

I told him I returned to LA and was so impacted with the experience that I wrote my first song entitled, "Emma Torres."

"Did you ever sing the song anywhere?" he asked.
"No," I told him.
"Do you think you will?"
"I don't know," I replied, "Maybe."
"Bah-ree, don't sing the song, just tell me the words."
So I did.

Well I drove down to Rosarito, Mexico,
Searching for my one true love.
It was a popular Mexican holiday,
Searching for my one true love,
Oh Emma Torres, where can you be?
Emma Torres, where can you be?

I met her at a festival, a year had come and gone,
We even danced a nice slow dance.
Although we didn't talk about coming back the next year,
I figured she loved me as much as I loved her.
Oh Emma Torres, where can you be?
Emma Torres, where can you be?

No, I couldn't find Emma Torres,
I couldn't find her anywhere.
No, I couldn't find Emma Torres,
I couldn't find her anywhere.

Now I'm back here in the city,
Thinking about my one true love,
Working a job I could care less about,
Dreaming about my one true love,

Emma Torres, where can you be?
Emma Torres, where can you be?

No, I couldn't find Emma Torres,
I couldn't find her anywhere.
No, I couldn't find Emma Torres,
I couldn't find her anywhere.

After telling Casabubu the lyrics, he walked away, shaking his head from side to side. I'm pretty sure I heard him repeating, "Lock him up, what else can you do, lock him up."

Here and There

Romeo, Romeo, Where Art Thou?

June 11, 2003

A couple of Saturdays ago, Air France's Concorde flew from New York to Paris for the last time. I never flew on it. Never even came close.

As you may know, the Concorde was the most luxurious and fastest of all airplanes, flying at twice the speed of sound.

I wonder if Superman flew that fast.

I hope so.

In a recent Utica *Observer-Dispatch* newspaper article, the chief financial officer of Michelin Tires in Thailand said about the Concorde, "There's a lot of luxury. You're eating the most beautiful food, drinking the most beautiful wine. You can't compare it to anything, even to first class."

One woman, on a monthly basis, bought a seat on the Concorde for herself and her dog Romeo.

Can you imagine? Romeo had his own seat on the Concorde. Every month, yet. I never flew in an airplane first class. Romeo, a dog, has me beat. That's a little rough.

A friend and I – back in my college days – hitchhiked through Europe. On the way back from Lisbon to New York, the airline messed up our reservations, and, to make up for it, gave us seats in a private space between first class and economy. It was a small section sort of by itself with a table that separated us. That was the closest I came to first class.

Luxury? Let's see.

One time, when I lived in New York, a friend of mine, Ronnie Mevs from Haiti, had a friend who came into the restaurant we both worked at, where we happened to be hanging out at the time. Excitedly, he told Ronnie he was driving an old Rolls Royce and had it parked outside, offering to take us for a ride.

You could say we made a "lightning-quick" decision to comply. We then sat in the back seat, high up in that old beautiful Rolls. We felt so important as we were driven around our neighborhood, laughing all the while.

So now that the Concorde is no longer going back and forth to Paris, that's one luxury I won't have to wish for.

Phew.

I was once given a tour through a small candy factory that was for sale in New England. It was right out of Roald Dahl's famous book, *Willy Wonka and the Chocolate Factory.*

Candy was – everywhere – in boxes, in trays on shelves cooling on carts – with chocolate dripping from them. Luxury?

Pretty close.

I once bought a new car. The night that happened, I felt luxurious. And poorer.

Is too much of anything not good? Conventional wisdom says yes. That means flying on a Concorde too many times, eating and drinking all the beautiful food and drink you want, ruins that luxury? Well, I guess I'll never know.

The real question is, now that there are no more Concorde airplane trips back and forth to and from Paris, will Romeo ever be the same?

I'll leave that for the canine psychologists to ponder.

A Guinness World Record Stomach

August 6, 2003

Here are some observations and questions from our family's recent vacation to York Beach, Maine:

I saw a seagull that limped.

Where do all the little rocks on the beach come from? Millions of them.

The way the ocean tide is "in" or "out" is fascinating. Keeps you on your toes.

Finding a good pizza is not easy, wherever you are (except Boonville).

Parents should teach their shrieking children not to do that. Mine never did.

Well, maybe once.

I've never eaten so much ice cream in my life.

The sun is better than the rain.

Good, hot buttered blueberry muffins ... are divine.

I saw a Ford Expedition that was bigger than North America.

Being mailed a *Boonville Herald* in Maine was very exciting, particularly since my column was in it.

There's nothing like your own refrigerator.

There's absolutely nothing like your own bathroom.

And there is positively, unquestionably, absolutely, unequivocally, nothing ... like your own bed.

Mosquitoes are annoying wherever you are.

You're never really very far from a discarded cigarette butt.

You watch television wherever you are.

When you eat lobster, even with a bib on, you still get "it" over you. Just less.

How can a telephone pole suddenly be washed up on the rocks? A telephone pole!

There's something about a surfer. I wouldn't go out there all alone with just a piece of wood or plastic, no matter what.

I met a beagle early one morning while writing on the beach. Its name was Dusty Rose. I was told everyone knew her as Dusty.

Some women, and, of course some men, shouldn't wear bathing suits. I saw a man wearing one whose stomach hung over his bathing trunks. I've never seen anything like it. It looked like a very large nose. Put a top on! It's a wonder he didn't topple over. I have no comments on the women. None I can tell … and live.

On the way back from Maine, at a rest stop on the Massachusetts Turnpike, there were more people there than there are at the Kentucky Derby.

Vacations "go by" like a flash.

Being lazy on your vacation is terrific.

Even if you're not on vacation, it's not so bad at home.

Dogs and Cats of the World, Let's Talk

September 3, 2003

There's a Japanese toy company that manufactures the world's first dog-human translation gadget. A dog barks and a small microphone the dog wears translates that bark to a palm-sized electronic device, whose small screen tells you what the dog is saying. Now sold in U.S. stores, it's called "Bowlingual".

The company collected tapes of "voices" from 2,000 dogs and found patterns that changed with emotions. When the dog barks into the microphone attached to its collar, the gadget analyzes it into: frustration, menace, demand, joy, sorrow and self-expression. For instance, if sad, the dog barks and on the screen appears, "Please, don't forget me!"

They're working on one for cats, to be called "Meowlingual". I suppose it's possible that, in time, we'll be able to communicate with cats. Here's a possible "Meowlingual" scenario.

Fluffy, tell me, what's on your mind?

"Sick."

What do you mean sick? You're not feeling well?

"No, not that kind of sick, I'm sick of … you. And, as long as we're talking about it, I'm not entirely thrilled with the rest of your family."

But why? We treat you so well. You eat like a kin… I mean, queen. You have a clean house to roam in, water all the time, frequent catnip … what have we denied you?

"I want a four-poster bed."

Somehow that doesn't surprise me, Fluff.

Cats are something else.

So folks, do you get the picture on where this whole communications thing could go? But don't let it be said I stood in the way of language progress.

Let's continue.

Fluffy, what would you like the posters adorning your bed to be made of?

"Pure gold and nothing less."

Pure gold ... huh ... why you ungrat ... aw, never mind. So Fluff, I know I shouldn't ask you, but ... what else would you like, now that we can speak through "Meowlingual"?

"Don't talk to me unless I talk to you."

You're treading on shaky ground, Fluff. In any event, please know this, my dear Queen Cateeva. It would be most wise of you not to bite the hand that literally feeds you. You get my drift?

"Yes, boss."

That's what I like about you, Fluff. When it comes right down to it, you know where your bread's buttered. Now I know you're moody, like some fem ... ahhhh ... animals, so I'll cut you some slack. But please, mind your manners, OK?

"Fine. Now be off with you."

There you go again.

Now this conversation may never happen. But, in trying to understand all this sophisticated electronic business about communicating with dogs, maybe it'll be some time before they perfect "Meowlingual".

How about – if I'm lucky, not in my lifetime!

Some would say, "Aw, you love cats deep down, don't you? Come on, admit it!"

All I can say to that is, just thinking about it makes me itch.

So know that, as technology in the form of "Bowlingual" and "Meowlingual" devices creep forward, it gives us new insight into what Fidos and Fluffys out there might be telling us.

I don't think I want to know.

Well-Deserved Role Models

September 17, 2003

We all have our role models.

I grew up watching Roy Rogers cowboy films. Recently seeing a TV special on him, well … it got me.

So I did some research.

Three months after Roy was born in Cincinnati, Ohio, his family moved to Portsmouth, Ohio. For seven years, they lived on a houseboat Roy's father and uncle built for them.

Can you imagine living on a houseboat for the first seven years of your life?

They then bought a small farm raising, as Roy later said, "Rocks". His father worked 100 miles away in Cincinnati at a shoe factory, coming home on weekends, while Roy ran the farm.

Roy's mother, Mattie, was lame from polio.

Roy often rode Babe, an old sulky racehorse to school. Roy sang, played mandolin and guitar, called square dances and yodeled. His mother would yodel to him when he was in the fields when a storm was coming, when lunch had arrived and when to come in at the end of the day.

He quit high school in his second year to work with his father in the shoe factory. They both, shortly thereafter, quit and drove their rickety family car to California where Roy's oldest sister lived with her husband. The car, which barely made it, is in their famous museum in California.

Roy ended up picking peaches in the same labor camps John Steinbeck wrote about in his book, and later portrayed in the film, *The Grapes of Wrath*.

At Roy's sister's place in California, after hearing Roy play and sing with the guitar, she convinced him to try out for an appearance on a midnight radio talent show. Three days after appearing on the show, he was asked to join a small country singing group.

The group ended up in Roswell, New Mexico, where they were interviewed on a radio station promoting an appearance they were to perform at. They had run out of money and were literally starving.

During the interview, Roy purposely said he missed his mom's lemon pie, hoping someone would pick up the hint. A caller responded requesting Roy sing and yodel, promising two lemon pies if he did. He more than gladly complied.

That night, the caller, and her daughter Arlene, knocked on Roy's motel door and delivered the two pies. When back in Los Angeles, Roy corresponded with Arlene, marrying her years later. That marriage produced an adopted daughter. They had a second daughter, but one week later after that daughter's birth, his wife died of an embolism while still in the hospital.

Roy started doing pictures with Dale Evans and four years later married her.

They had a girl of their own and over a period of years, adopted an American Indian girl, a young boy from a welfare home, a girl from a Scotland orphanage, and an orphaned Korean girl.

Roy's only adopted son – while in his twenties – died in his sleep while in the Army in Germany.

At approximately the same time, their adopted 12-year-old Korean daughter died with her best friend in a fiery, tragic bus and car crash while driving back on their church bus after delivering toys and gifts to the poor in Tijuana, Mexico.

On the TV special I recently saw, Roy remarked that he and Dale had to have faith to have gotten through what they did with the deaths of their children.

It's been frequently said that losing a child is the worst thing a parent can endure. Did you ever see Roy or Dale with anything but smiles on their faces? They lived their lives with the same integrity depicted in their pictures.

I've looked long and hard for someone to emulate. I found two.

They're out there. You just have to find them.

A Shark! Holey Moley!

August 11, 2004

My wife, up to the time it was decision-time, had been resistant to doing it. My daughter and son were eager to do it. Me? I led the charge for it.

Pointing to my daughter and son, I told the man giving out the equipment, "It's just the three of us," and looking at my wife, continued, "But not my wife."

She then surprisingly said, "I'm going with you."

I was ecstatic, for up to that moment, I had been unable to encourage her to join us.

About 30 of us were then driven out on a decent-sized boat to where it would happen. The water was gorgeous, clear light blue. The guide explained to us how to use the equipment we had all been given. It took about 25 minutes to get out there. When we arrived, the motor to the boat was shut off.

From the back of the boat, each of us jumped into the warm azure water. With our life-vests keeping us buoyant, we treaded water, waiting for the rest on the boat to jump in.

When in the water, as the others were jumping in, I tried it out. I had the 12-inch yellow plastic tube in my mouth as earlier directed by our guide. Putting my head just below the water line, I breathed into the tube, with the other end sticking out of the water.

Alas, it worked! I was breathing underwater, viewing through a mask a crystal clear sea of water 40 feet down to the bottom. It was unlike anything I had ever previously seen.

When we were all in the water, the guide announced we were to begin, instructing us to follow him and to generally stay close to everyone there.

Viewing an exciting world of underwater life, we were snorkeling in the magnificent waters of Cancun, Mexico.

There was a prominence of yellow-streaked fish ranging in size up to 10 inches, which at first were visible in a "here-and-there" fashion. They were long and narrow and quite beautiful to look at.

At one point, as we followed our guide, I found myself next to my son Deane. Suddenly, the yellow fish we had sporadically seen, were all around us. So much so that all you had to do was stick your hand out, to seemingly touch them. That was thrilling.

Our guide would sporadically dive 40 feet to the bottom in a graceful fashion and when there, would look around those underwater bushes, seeking to dislodge a larger fish.

He repeated that routine perhaps a dozen times as we wended our way to where he knew they generally would be. For the first 10 or so times, he came up … ahhhh … empty-handed. No pun intended.

And then, on one of his dive attempts, when we least expected it, suddenly one emerged. He pointed to it with his arms in a sweeping fashion for all of us above to see, as an approximately seven-foot, fat, impressive shark appeared from the undergrowth and swam 30 feet or so in front of him. The shark then disappeared into a cluster of underwater foliage.

Me oh my!

And, now on to conquering Mount Everest.

And then rhino in the African bush.

Well, maybe not.

Oh all right …. not!

The Damsky Federales in Cancun, Mexico, 2004
(L-R, Deane, Melissa, Cynthia and yours truly)

There It Is, Hope!

August 24, 2004

Since I had emailed the hotel before going there, asking if they had one, their affirmative response only left one question unanswered – where was it?

The night we arrived at the hotel in Cancun, Mexico, on our family's recent vacation, not having unpacked, I walked around the hotel and it didn't take long for me to locate it. Next to the main lobby were two glass doors. Going through them, I found a small inner lobby that bordered their main conference room.

In that inner lobby, there it was, in a lonely corner – the hotel's grand piano. I tried it out to see how it sounded. It was considerably out-of-tune, probably because of Mexico's constant summer high humidity. Conspicuously absent was a piano bench.

As I glanced around to see what I could sit on to play it with when a better time presented itself, observing only the usual lobby furniture had me momentarily baffled. I sensed the only solution was to go into the adjoining conference room and borrow a chair from what I guessed to be the many there.

The next day, very early in the morning, I tried entering the main conference room to get a chair, only to find those doors locked.

A few days before we were to leave, "destiny smiled". It was 5:30 in the morning and still pretty dark. I tried one of the enormous doors to the conference room and it was open! I entered it and borrowed a chair from what looked like thousands set up, excitedly returning to the inner lobby with it to sit in the traditional manner before the piano.

It was getting light slowly, enough to be able to see what I then wrote on the yellow pad I had brought for that purpose, placing it on the piano's music stand.

I then started playing

An original musical melody emerged almost immediately, with equally as fresh words that seemed to fit it so well. A new song materialized quite easily, not always the case when I write songs.

I heard some light footsteps and turning around, saw a hotel worker approaching me.

He spoke only Spanish and having taken it in high school, that's what we spoke. I asked him if it was all right to use the piano and he vigorously smiled, signaling me it was.

I told him I had been writing songs for the past 12 years, all in the gospel vein, and the one he heard me doing, was what I so far had just written. I then sang him what I had, first singing each line in English and then saying that line in Spanish as best I could.

When I finished what I had, he commented that it was beautiful. Encouraged, I told him that, thus far, my songs had not been commercially successful, further explaining I felt one reason was that so far I was unable to position myself to find backup gospel singers for the songs.

I don't know what made me then say in my broken Spanish, "Perhaps God is telling me that this song I'm now writing will become successful in Spanish here in Mexico, and that it will be the break for the rest of my songs."

His smiling response I'll never forget. I didn't need to be expert in any language to have interpreted that.

He told me he played the guitar and that he and his wife sang in his church choir.

Now that I'm home, far from Mexico, I've been refining the song, singing half of it in Spanish after having found a couple of web sites that change English into Spanish. The last remaining task is getting a green light from someone who is expert in Spanish to make sure the grammar is correct.

So it's onward to play out life's plan for the song, if any.

By the way, so far, that Cancun song is entitled, "You're An Old Friend."

The first line is, "You're an old friend I can count on, all the time."

Some Toreador

June 29, 2005

The summer preceding my senior year at Utica College, with my friend Alan Goldman about to enter his first year at Syracuse Law School, we decided to go on a last summer adventure, hitchhiking through England, France and Spain. Our trip included spending the entire eight days of the annual Fiesta De San Fermin, more familiarly known as the Running of the Bulls, in Pamplona, Spain.

It was just like it was portrayed both in Ernest Hemingway's novel *The Sun Also Rises* and the movie of the same name.

For the entire eight days, it was 24-hour-a-day dancing, drinking, singing and parades in the streets, highlighted with daily bullfights and religious ceremonies.

At eight each morning, four bulls and four cows (to keep the bulls calm), were all let out of their pens, rambling for several minutes through a barricaded street-course leading directly into the bullring. When there, the animals were ushered out the other side of the arena to their pens, where, later that afternoon, those four bulls would meet their ultimate fate at the bullfights.

Preceding the animals from the pens to the bull ring ran brave adventurers, thrill-seekers and a goodly percentage of fools. Those runners ended up assembled on the dirt floor of the bullfight arena for what happened next, as one at a time, small bulls with taped horns were then let into the bullring. That's when the fun really began.

Alan and I wanted to experience the running with the bulls part, but didn't want to risk life and limb with the possibility we'd get trampled and hurt – perhaps permanently – by all that street-running craziness.

We figured if we positioned ourselves behind the wooden barricade on the street, as the animals went by, we'd count the bulls and cows and then duck through the barrier. We'd then run after them into the bullring before they closed the gigantic doors.

Valor in reverse.

The second day there, our plan worked. We were two of the last people to get through those massive doors before they clanked shut.

We were in!

I can remember it, oh so clearly. I stood on that hallowed arena dirt floor where so many famous bullfighters had stood before me. Alan and I were smack in the middle of the mass of runners who had previously run with the bulls. Topping it all off in the arena stands was the bulging, murmuring crowd. They looked down at all of us, knowing what was about to happen. It was, without a doubt, one of the most exciting moments of my life.

It was only because of the sudden roar of the crowd that we figured a young bull was let out. Then, it was amateur bullfighter time. Because there were so many people on the floor of the arena, we couldn't tell where the bull was.

We were tipped off only when the mass of those on the floor parted like a sea. And, there it was … a formidable looking bull you didn't want to mess with, taped horns or not. Alan and I both ran for the safety of the inner barrier that circled the inside of the arena. When there, I stammered, "We must be brave and get out there."

A few moments later, I heard the crowd roar, and looking up, saw a person near me tossed by the bull – perfectly – head over heels. As he got up, I yelled, "Alan, wow, did you see that? Alan! Alan, where are you?" The person that had been tossed was walking toward me as I was still yelling for Alan.

And, as he approached me, I then stunningly realized … it was Alan!

"Why did you do that?" I asked incredulously.

With glazed eyes he responded, "You just got through telling me we had to be brave."

I then squeaked, "You didn't have to do what I said."

The next day, with vindication as my inspiration, I awoke early, asking Alan if he wanted to accompany me to the early morning spectacle again.

I heard a barely audible, "No."

So I went by myself, and following the previous day's plan, successfully got into the arena with relative ease.

Given that second chance, I forced myself to stay in the middle of the mass on the bullfight floor. After the first young bull was released, it wasn't long before the sea of people parted and there it was. It was very frightening looking.

It stopped no more than 15 feet from where I stood. I was on one side of the enclosed circle that suddenly formed around us and the young bull was on the other. I've never been quite as "frozen with fear" as I was at that moment. Someone waved a shirt at him to get his attention, and suddenly, he was gone.

Was I vindicated?

More than the previous day.

At this time of year, I look back on that type of excitement with more than casual interest as the Pamplona reports appear in the papers and on television.

I suspect Alan does, too, from Phoenix where he lives.

All I can say is – Ole! – I think...

A True Heroine

November 16, 2005

What makes a person a part of heroic history to be remembered, perhaps forever? How are certain people chosen for that lofty status?

Some African-American had to say "no" along life's way when ordered by a bus driver to go sit in the back.

Rosa Parks, who died recently, was designated 50 years ago this coming December, to be that person.

And with her "no" to that bus driver's dictate in Montgomery, Alabama, Rosa exposed the racial and legal prejudice and bigotry amongst man, prevalent at the time, exposing it for the ignorance and disease it was. And, although just the first step, she blasted it into this country's consciousness for all to see.

Did Rosa have more courage than most of us?

She had to.

We all have our boiling points, our overflows, our … I-can't-take-it-anymores!

Rosa had hers.

In November 1956, 12 months after Rosa's simple act of heroism, the highest court in the land ruled that transportation segregation was unconstitutional.

And all because of Rosa Parks, who died this past October 24th.

Some days after her death, 30 thousand faithful in Washington paid their respects by also walking by her casket, history itself, as Rosa became the first woman of any color to lie in such honor in the nation's Capitol rotunda.

Do we all have in us the qualities to stand up for what is right as Rosa did? I sure hope so.

Each and every one of us know the injustices against us and humanity – Little Montgomerys – and yet, why don't most of us speak out when ignorance is foisted upon us, as it was against Rosa, before she couldn't take it anymore? If Rosa, who lived to be 92, didn't teach us anything by her incredible life, shame on us.

Let her life serve as an inspiration for all humanity, so when we see wrongs in this amazing journey of life, we must – as she did – stand up for its counterpart – the right of correctness to prevail.

In our lifetime, we've seen the courage and strength of a Rosa Parks. What a privilege to have lived in her time. How very precious was her dignity, grace, courage – and by her action – her hope.

May we never forget her, so that her memory will be a constant spur against those who side with injustice, side with wrong.

It's really quite incredible, for all she did to alter history, was utter one rather tiny word – "No."

What an amazing lesson.

Can't Be That Much Farther To Heaven

January 4, 2006

When you get on the elevator to go up 67 floors – as soon as the door closes and you start moving up – heavy upbeat music starts playing, accompanied by flashing lights from the elevator ceiling. Looking up at the lights, you can also see through the top of the elevator at the shaft you're going up at a most respectable speed. The ascent is particularly smooth as is the gradual slowdown arriving at the top.

In early December of last year, less than a month ago, I saw on *The Today Show* how they opened up the top couple of floors to tourists of Rockefeller Center in New York City. It's called "Top of the Rock".

It used to be open to the public many years ago, but it was closed to tourists, so opening it up recently struck me as a big deal.

Knowing that my wife, daughter, son and I were all going to be in New York on a one-day bus trip to see the Rockefeller Center Christmas Show, it seemed a natural to take in the "Top of the Rock" tour.

We looked it up on the web and purchased tickets on the internet the night before the trip.

As you exit the elevator on the 67th floor, you can look out the windows on all four sides and can go outside to the open deck and do the same. Elevators also take you up two flights from there, where you are officially at the "Top of the Rock".

We had miscalculated how long it would take us to go through the lines and procedures ... it was as if you were going through airport security. We had, time-wise, the choice to check out the four direction views from the lobby of the 67th floor, plus being able to go outside, or, wait in line to take the elevator to the 69th floor.

Since we had to be at the Christmas Spectacular on the ground floor and didn't have much time to get there, we opted for the 67th floor choice. Looking out from the inside, was an unforgettable experience.

Looking down, from that high up, literally took my breath away. I didn't walk over to the very edge of the windows; rather, I held back a decent foot because I noticed that the closer I got to the edge to look down (and don't forget I'm on the inside), it was downright frightening.

I wondered how anyone could build a building that tall, going against all supposed sanity and logic.

While on the outside deck, I noticed that the Empire State Building was located very close to where we were and viewing it from that high up was spectacular. My daughter took a picture of it that is most dramatic. The picture clearly shows the stunning Statue of Liberty in the background.

It is not only worth the trip to see the incredible Empire State Building that close, that far up, but a great life experience.

It also makes me want to go see the film *King Kong*.

Who Meets a Famous Mother?

March 15, 2006

At a recent Sunday morning gospel brunch in Myrtle Beach, South Carolina, the lead singer of the group "Glory", with a wireless microphone, would frequently walk through those in attendance at the club, *House of Blues*. He would sing whatever song most knew and engaged those he strolled by to sing along with him.

In one instance, while singing "This Little Light of Mine," he approached a long table of ten, and stopped there, a sign they were chosen. Some at that table accepted the challenge by standing up and singing the main chorus as the musicians played on. At that table was a smartly dressed African-American woman. At the end of the song, he stood by her, holding a plate over his head with something on it. He announced there was a celebrity in the house who had a birthday. As soon as he said it, the woman he was standing next to smiled radiantly. I turned to my wife and remarked, "That woman has such a beautiful smile."

The singer then announced, "The birthday of today's celebrity is … Mrs. Rose Rock, the mother of Chris Rock." He then said that what he had on the plate he held over his head, was not a birthday cake, but "A genuine South Carolina blueberry muffin."

By that time, my wife, her mother and I had finished our brunch, and the two of them decided to go shopping nearby, leaving me there to enjoy the music.

Later, as I was waiting in the lobby for them to pick me up, Rose Rock came out with her coat draped over her arm. To put it on, she put down a small package on the floor right next to where I happened to be standing. As she did so, I took a step toward her and said, "You must be a brilliant woman to have raised such an accomplished son, knowing the apple doesn't fall far from the tree." Blushing with humility, she replied, "Oh, I don't know about that, but that's very nice of you to say." That dazzling smile appeared as she continued, "I may have had a little bit to do with it."

As we further talked, I asked her where they lived as Chris grew up. She responded, "Brooklyn." I inquired if she was involved at that time with anything other than raising her family. She told me she was a teacher in the New York City school system and that her husband worked for the *New York Times*. I asked her in what capacity. She replied that he was a truck driver and had since passed away.

She was one of those people that, when you talked to them, you felt you knew them for a long time. She told me that Chris currently was narrating his current TV series *Everybody Hates Chris* and that he lived in Los Angeles and New Jersey. And, that one of her other sons, Tony, also lived in Los Angeles and is starring in his own TV series, *All of Us*. She further mentioned that she had two other younger sons who were, referring to Chris and Tony's TV accomplishments, "waiting in the wings."

I told her that before the singer had introduced her, I had mentioned her great smile to my wife. She thanked me graciously and her lady friend, who was listening to our conversation, put her arm around her and said, "That's our Rose."

Several days later, I went to the Myrtle Beach Library, and on the internet, found some of the following about her son Chris:
Born in 1965.
Standup comic for 12 years.
Had his film debut in *Beverly Hills Cop II*.
On the television cast of *Saturday Night Live* for three years.
Married with two children.
Eddie Murphy discovered him.

Has two comedy albums.

Has his star in the "Hollywood Walk of Fame".

Hosted the 2005 77th Academy Awards.

His mother is Rose Rock.

Oh, Rose told me she lived in the Los Angeles and Myrtle Beach areas.

I should have asked her how her "genuine South Carolina blueberry muffin" tasted.

Only in New York

May 24, 2006

On a late afternoon two Saturdays ago, my wife and a couple of friends from the bus tour we had taken from Boonville earlier that morning, were wasting a half-hour leaning against a wall on Broadway in New York City's theatre district. The theatre, where we'd soon see a musical, was nearby.

Way up high on a building on the other side of Broadway, for easily half a city block wide, was a gigantic billboard that heralded the musical play, *Mama Mia*. The sign, besides its enormity, was quite simple. It read: *MAMA MIA* – A SMASH HIT MUSICAL BASED ON THE SONGS OF ABBA – AT THE WINTER GARDEN THEATRE."

To say it stood out was an understatement. We all wondered how much a sign of that incredible magnitude would cost. I made a note to call Paul Panara – who I deal with in my advertising agency work – when I got back home. He heads a billboard company in Utica.

Suddenly, just feet from us, appeared a mime in white face and dirty orange construction clothes. He stood in one fixed position on a crude wooden box with a hat in front of him on the sidewalk for anyone to contribute their financial appreciation for his performance. When someone would put money in his hat, he would mechanically break his "frozen" character, look at them in his vice-like manner, and wink. He would keep that look for a short time and then revert to his previous locked position. He was quite good.

The play we then went to see was the musical *Wicked*. I've

never seen a play that drew me in as much as that one did. With the superb acting, plus the incredible music with the usual Broadway technical wizardry, well – it was one of the best plays I've seen.

The two female leads the play revolved around gave breathless performances. One of them, Megan Hilty, is a graduate of Carnegie Mellon University in Pittsburgh, famous alone for its prestigious drama department. Until *Wicked*, Megan was in just three plays, rather incredible for the star she now is because of the play's success. Her comic timing in the play was brilliant, her voice as good as it gets, and her acting of the highest caliber. Usually, it takes more than three plays to develop the skills to reach such a lofty esthetic level. She's a true performing phenomenon.

After the show, when our bus tour was eating at B.B. King's Restaurant and Blue's Club on famed 42nd Street, when everyone at our table had received their main dish except my wife, I got a waiter's attention.

Pointing to my wife's empty space where her main dish should have been, I declared, "Salmon, she ordered salmon." The waiter looked questioningly at me as if I had spoken Greek. Boring on, figuring if I repeated it, he'd then understand, I again clearly repeated, "Salmon, she ordered salmon." His blank stare continued for what seemed an eternity. He finally took a stab and questioned, "Feesh?" I exclaimed, "Yes!" Shortly thereafter, he brought the salmon.

Feesh.

Oh – Paul Panara told me how much that mammoth *Mama Mia* outdoor board costs to rent. Depending on the sign's bells and whistles, it goes between 120 and 160 thousand dollars a month.

You read it right.

Unbelievable.

New York.

In a class by itself.

Two Ships in the Night

November 8, 2006

After Utica College, when I moved to New York City, my best friend in that acting phase of my life was Ron Mevs, a Haitian.

It was a period in both our lives when we were both trying to figure out what we'd do in life – me, thinking it was my destiny to be a working actor. Although discouraged because that wasn't happening, I did what I thought I should do to accomplish that. He was one of those friends who stayed the friendship course through those challenging times.

Towards the end of the eight years I lived in New York, I attended his first marriage in Harlem. Shortly thereafter, I left New York for California. About 35 surprising years later, my phone rang at my home in Boonville. It was Ron.

He and his second wife and their two children had to flee Haiti because of its unsettling political climate, choosing Montreal, Canada. About seven years ago my wife and I drove up there for a weekend to see them.

During all those years, Ron had slowly and successfully gained popularity as a working artist.

As the political climate eased, they returned to Haiti. A couple of months ago, Ron's wife emailed me to come to Greenwich, Connecticut, for the opening of Ron's featured art show.

My wife couldn't make it, so I drove there, staying at my middle brother's house just minutes from Ron's show.

When I walked into the gallery featuring his paintings, the first person to greet me was Ron. And, it was at that moment – when we hugged each other – I knew he was one of those rare friends one is so blessed to have in life.

His wife and family arrived a bit later as well as two of his sons from his first marriage, both very handsome.

I learned from the owner of the gallery and others there that afternoon – and there were many – that Ron is one of Haiti's leading artists.

When the show concluded for the night, Ron, his wife and I went to a nearby restaurant. Sitting there with him, it was like old times in New York.

Before saying our farewells, we sat in my car and I played him several portions of songs that will be on the gospel CD I've been recording for the last year. I sang earlier in my New York days, but back then, neither of us knew of the importance his art or my singing and writing would later evolve to.

In the car, on the second song, he asked who it was that was singing and who wrote the songs. When I told him me, he quietly said, "Unbelievable." Ron always was – and remains to be – encouraging.

He and his wife mentioned that they were about to visit China for his art.

I told them, before I drove away from that parking lot in Greenwich, that they should come visit me and my wife in Boonville. He told me they definitely would, but since the nature of his business was such that he never knew where he was going next, he said, "We'll come when you least expect it."

So the "Ron-Mevs-Visiting-Boonville-Watch"... is officially on.

By the way, if you google "Haitian Artist Ron Mevs," it says, "Mevs, Ronald – One of Haiti's modern creative geniuses."

Land of the Dictator – Right There!

February 21, 2007

It was late morning and I was sitting by myself at the front of the cruise ship.

I was in one of their many night clubs, this one located at the front of the ship, with views through gigantic floor-to-ceiling windows on three sides surrounding the club. The ship was 13 floors high and the club was on the 12th floor.

It was only open for business at night, but you could walk in at any time of the day and sit anywhere you wished, which most didn't take advantage of. In the non-business hours, I enjoyed writing on my laptop computer in that private environment.

It was the morning of one of our last of five days on our maiden cruise when I heard my wife approach me from behind and excitedly whisper, "Look over there ... do you know what that is?"

I looked where she was pointing, and through the windows about 15 feet to my right, saw – what I was later told was 20 miles away – the misty outline of the Sierra del Rosario Mountains.

My wife then excitedly said, "It's Cuba."

I jumped up exclaiming, "Unbelievable! How do you know?"

"Everybody's talking about it. It's Cuba," she repeated with assurance.

It was a clear morning, but over the entire length of the left side of Cuba – as our cruise ship was travelling northward on our way back to Miami – hung an eerie misty cloud cover you could see through showing continuous mountains.

As we slowly passed by Cuba, that was the feeling I had

– eeriness – knowing it was a land where freedom was restricted. It was as if an invisible wall surrounded it, for not 20 miles away was a country headed by Fidel Castro, one of the most known dictators of modern time.

When attending the University of Miami in late 1957 – one memorable night – I returned to my dorm consisting of five other room-mates. I was immediately told, "We're all going to Cuba tonight and you're coming." I responded, "You can go to Cuba, but I'm not."

"It's cheap," they charged on. "We'll drive down to Key West and for about $15 round trip, we'll then fly to Havana where everything is cheap. We'll have a great time!"

I was resolute in my refusal to go, emphatically telling them to go and have a good time, but not with me.

Two hours later, there I sat in the back seat of one of their cars as we all drove the one way into Key West to fly from their airport – to Cuba.

So much for resoluteness.

And thus, a weekend ensued in Havana that was exciting and adventurous. It was an open city in those days, what with gambling in exquisite casinos, cheap food, fancy hotels and varied tourist attractions. It was a true foreign experience. Just the old vehicles alone – was an exciting step back in automotive time.

Little did we all know that, in but a couple of years, Fidel Castro would take power and rule with an iron hand to the present.

My wife and I went to the top deck of the ship and took pictures of what we could see of Cuba, as our ship slowly passed it by. I thought how so many had risked their lives over the years fleeing Cuba by boat in the dead of night for Florida.

To a much different way of life here in America.

To freedom.

I'm so thankful to live in these United States where I can leave the country if I want, as we did for our cruise. And among other "things," to be able to freely write these very words.

Not so in Cuba.

A classic lesson in gratefulness for the incredible preciousness of freedom.

Old Blue Eyes

March 26, 2008

My wife, mother-in-law and I recently visited Barefoot Landing, a shopping center in Myrtle Beach, South Carolina.

The way it was laid out, you had to go across one of two wooden walkways to get from one side of the shopping center to the other over about a hundred yards of water. When we went over the walkway – looking down 10 feet or so to the water below – we saw turtles, large fish and, although we didn't see any alligators, there were signs on the walkways that clearly stated to keep your hands away from the alligators … as they may bite.

That got our attention.

We walked into a jewelry store with a lone salesman. As we all looked at whatever took our fancy, my wife asked him a question concerning a piece of jewelry. He patiently and knowledgeably explained the answer to whatever it was she asked. He had beautiful, long white hair that looked most cool. He wore a simple but elegant black sweater over an equally simple and elegant white shirt – the effect which was most stylish. To top it all off, he had the bluest eyes I think I've ever seen on any human being.

I asked him how many years he had been in the jewelry business. He said, "I was 20 when I started."

He paused for a few moments and added, "I'll be 94 in November."

He explained that he filled in part-time at the jewelry store to keep busy.

He was as sharp and entertaining as any human being of any age.

He told me he opened up his first jewelry store in New York City on 5th Avenue and 14th Street.

I told him that area was my old "stomping grounds" when I first moved to New York after college.

While talking to him – every once in a while – I'd catch a waft of the cologne he was wearing. And when that happened, it was momentarily mesmerizing.

He told me he was a singer and horn player before entering the jewelry business, and when in Canada for a short period of time, had organized his own band. When he was about to return to the United States, the piano player of his group – whose piano virtuosity he described as nothing short of great – came to him and excitedly told him he was going to venture out on his own as a solo piano player ... further mentioning he was going to change his full name to one word only.

I guessed, "Liberace?"

He replied, "Yes."

He was an absolutely fascinating man to talk to.

You should have seen his blue eyes.

Canine Superiority?

April 9, 2008

So … I'm driving on the New York State Thruway on the way to Syracuse … and a van passes me with a sticker on the back stating, "Caution, Show Dogs Aboard."

I thought about how I should be particularly careful not to go near that vehicle because … it carries show dogs and because that sticker sends a signal to us humans … we're in second place.

Dogs first … and – for the rest of us – who cares?

It's good we all know where we stand.

Second place to a show dog … hmmmnnn …

I've never had personal experience with a show dog, but I can only guess that they've worked long and hard learning the rigors of control necessary to compete. And the least they can expect for that, is vehicle-sticker recognition.

When you see them on television at dog shows with their masters leading them around the ring, it's quite impressive to see how they are so well-disciplined. Let's face it, those show dogs have put in some heavy training time.

Now, I don't pretend to be an expert on show dogs. Some of them appear to "march" better than others and their grooming seems to be impeccable. And you see breeds that are so unique. They obviously deserve the accolades and ribbons they receive.

And they have to be pure, registered with the omnipotent dog organization that checks that kind of "stuff". Pure. We humans can't claim that. We'd never be able to be "shown" like dogs because of that alone.

"What's that, sir, do I have 'papers'?"

Only the ones delivered every morning.

Oh, that's not good enough?

Sorry. Guess I can't compete.

So the next time you see a sticker on a van announcing we're in the passing presence of one or more show dogs – gosh – you'll know you've been around celebrity.

After all, what have we humans done that could hold up to what show dogs have accomplished?

At the risk of having show dog masters aim their furious fingers at us humans … in particular, me, haven't we studied more, invested more than what dogs have accomplished?

And we're human, right?

Just checking.

The fact we're not led around on a leash, isn't that a clue? Come to think of it, I have seen relationships where one partner may as well be.

Now I'm not impugning any of the doggies that are so smart, so handsome or beautiful … and whose masters have the time and money to invest in the whatever-size Fidos … who proudly prance around a horizontal track … strutting their stuff before adoring fans. They are something to behold. They sure deserve the ribbons the elite of the pack are awarded.

All I'm saying is … somebody – please – slap a sticker on our vehicles rewarding us humans for … something!

Like, "Humans On Board, Feed!"

I'd like to think the late comedian Rodney Dangerfield would have said about us humans, "We don't get any respect."

Aren't we worth just one vehicle sticker?

Come on!

He Found Me. What Are the Odds of That?

September 24, 2008

So I'm shaving and into my mind pops Sitges, Spain. Don't ask me why.

It was 1964, the summer of my junior year at Utica College. My friend and I were traveling via hitchhiking in Europe. We had bought a popular book, *Europe On $5 a Day*, and pretty much lived by it. I don't think you could do that today.

We were in Sitges, Spain, a beautiful small town on the Mediterranean Sea, staying at what the Spanish called a "pension," their version of what we know as a bed and breakfast. My friend and I were having breakfast when a tall gentleman walked in with the woman who ran the pension. She pointed to me and said, "That's him." He looked at me and replied, "No, that's not him." He then hesitantly said to me in a questionable manner, "Barry, is that you?"

I answered, "Joel?"

Seven years earlier, I attended the University of Miami. There were six of us in our apartment. My room-mate was Joel Davidson, from Passaic, New Jersey. Joel led the charge when we went to Cuba.

After the only year I spent at the University of Miami, a couple of summers later, I visited Joel in Passaic. He arranged a "date" for me and we all went to some local night spot dancing the night away.

He even came to Utica a summer later, and I reciprocated a date for him and it was just like old times.

When he walked in out of the blue in Sitges, I asked him how he found me. He said he met a couple of girls on the beach who said they had just met a couple of guys from the United States staying at a pension, one named Barry from New York.

Not that there were that many, but he must have gone to every pension until he found me.

What do you think are the chances of that happening so many years later, after not being in touch with him, and on the skimpy statement of a girl on a beach many thousands of miles away in a small town in Spain?

That's what I thought about when I was recently shaving.

What happened to Joel Davidson?

Years later, after Sitges, he called me – once in Utica just before I moved out to Los Angeles.

But nothing came out of the call, and I haven't heard or seen from him since.

I have a sense someday he'll reappear, probably based more on wishful thinking than anything else.

While working for the radio station here in Boonville, while on the air one afternoon, I told that Sitges, Spain, story of Joel and how it defied the odds how it all happened. Listeners called in about similar stories of incredible odds and it was most interesting. But none to match Joel finding me in Sitges, Spain.

(I finally tracked down Joel Davidson who was living in Knoxville, Tennessee. I would talk to him on my cell phone on the way home from my advertising agency business in Utica. He was an Army Airborne Ranger - Special Forces, and a Russian interpreter during the Viet Nam War. He was also a motivational speaker, teaching how to run installations at the Army Staff Management College in Kansas. He owned and ran a San Francisco club featuring the top rock acts of the 60's. He had Parkinson's disease and died in September of 2011. He was a good man and I deeply miss him to this day.)

We've Got to Leave - Now!

January 7, 2009

I have great memories as a child of taking the train with my parents from Utica to New York City. Sitting on the right-hand side of the train, as anyone knows who's taken that trip from Albany to the city, you see the mighty Hudson River that stays in view until arriving in the Big Apple.

We took that trip some weeks ago, with it being joyous in many ways. My wife, up to that time, had taken a train on one prior occasion, when our children were young and we all took a short Santa Claus train trip from Utica's train station.

As my wife sat next to the window on the train, she was dazzled by all that one sees looking at the Hudson River ... flying by at speeds which – we were told – reach 115 miles per hour during certain stretches along the way.

We stayed at a hotel in New York's theatre district, a half a block from Broadway, amidst all that sensationalism. No matter how many times I've seen it, it continues to dazzle me.

After shopping at Macy's – an experience in itself – we found ourselves on 8th Avenue as we walked back to our hotel. We saw a police car with flashing lights parked on the side we were on. As we walked by, there stood a policeman, nonchalantly facing the walk-by traffic, with a young man standing next to him with his back to us. What got my attention about the young man was that he had his hands clasped in back of him with handcuffs on. There was no excitement, no panic, no anything, just a quiet – what appeared to be normal – routine of the 8th Avenue flow.

We ate at a buffet-style eat in/take out restaurant next to our hotel. It had freshly-squeezed orange juice, a delicacy to me of immense proportions. In fact, as the evening progressed, I made plans to go there the next morning to take out some breakfast goodies, with the main thrust being their freshly-squeezed orange juice which I came close to dreaming about that night. That next morning, I went there, only to find that the woman standing in the check-out line before me had purchased the last container of orange juice.

I was "crushed", pun intended.

The day we left, we ate at a B.B. King's Sunday brunch at his blues club on 42nd Street that featured the Harlem Gospel Choir. At home, I had previously looked that situation up on the internet and learned that one could interact with that group's singers after they performed.

Sitting next to us – at our table – was a couple from Manchester, England. I briefly mentioned to the wife of that couple that I recently completed a CD of my gospel music. I also mentioned that I brought a couple of them in hopes of getting them to the singers for their possible performing/recording interest.

The singers had great voices; the total sound and presentation was truly powerful gospel music.

As the program progressed, my wife and I suddenly realized that – if we were to make our train back home – we would have to leave right then and there. As we said our hasty farewells, the British woman offered to take my CDs to the singers when they had completed their singing. I gratefully gave them to her.

Ah … New York City – always full of surprises.

True Love

March 18, 2009

On our recent vacation to Bonita Beach, Florida – on a nearby beach – my wife and I dug a hole for our beach umbrella in the crusty, seashell-laden sand, and settled in. We then observed the Gulf Coast birds that flew and strolled by and generally went about their usual lifestyle business.

From time to time, pelicans – the dark colored kind – would float about. But it was a beautiful white snowy egret, about 18 inches high, that got our attention. We didn't know if it was a he or a she, but we decided – because of its behavior – it was a male, naming it Iggy.

Beach passers-by would stop and look at it as it stood motionless gazing out at the ocean not appearing to be fazed by the attention it was getting.

So what's such a big deal about that particular snowy egret?

It stayed around.

We were there for several hours and it was still there when we left, not moving one inch.

But it was the way it was there that captured our attention.

At first, as it stood there, I mused that it had a date at noon – which is when we arrived – and, as time went on, I'd tell my wife, "His date is late."

We then guessed what Iggy was thinking as he stood there waiting. Here are some of those thoughts:

"She's late. Where could she be? But I love her and I'll gladly wait."

As my wife collected sea shells, as I lay on the beach chair under our umbrella shielding me from the sun, I'd glance over at Iggy and sure enough, there he was, motionless – still waiting.

When my wife returned from one of her trips along the beach with handfuls of shells she had no more room to hold, she, of course, noticed him. I commented what I thought Iggy was thinking:

"I'll always love you and dedicate my life to you no matter how long it takes for you to get here, even if I die right here on the spot. Yes, I love you beyond words."

Iggy just stood there – waiting – for hours.

Some other guessed Iggy thoughts:

"Of all the loves of my life, it's you I truly care for; so much so, that I dedicate every second of my life, to you."

"My mother wouldn't be happy if she knew you were so late, but she's dead."

"I never knew my father."

"My brothers and sisters don't really care … they haven't come by to see me in years."

"Oh, my darling, when will you arrive? I'm getting hungry,"

And when my wife and I broke beach camp, just before leaving, I gave a last glance at Iggy, as he gazed out to the Gulf Coast horizon.

We have some new expressions from that experience:

"Loyal as a snowy egret."

"Iggy loyal."

My outlook on life is broader because of Iggy. It gives me new perspective on patience.

I wonder if he's still waiting.

Floating Almost Magically

November 25, 2009

I hadn't seen my cousin Elaine, or her husband, since her mother's funeral in Utica some 10 years ago.

We were on a tour, and the plan was for my wife and me to spend a free day with them. They were to pick us up at our hotel, which they did.

It was late morning and the traffic was creeping along. It was as challenging as I've ever seen traffic anywhere, and we were told it was that way most of the time. We inched along and finally made it through the congested traffic to the outskirts of the city, where evidence of the desert became more pronounced the further we went.

It took about an hour to get there, pulling into the parking lot by noon. It was a hot day and we found a canopied area with chairs facing the water. My cousin and her husband sat facing the shoreline, while my wife and I changed into our bathing suits.

We were told to slip into the water by sitting down in the shallow part and gently push off and then slowly lean on our backs as we glided into deeper water. We were warned not to get any water in our eyes and by no means were we to dunk our heads under water.

We followed those directions and when we pushed off and both leaned on our backs stretching out in the water with our heads up, it happened immediately. There we were, floating with no effort on our part, in the Dead Sea in Israel.

And what a unique experience that was. Our feet stuck up as the salt water had that supporting effect, holding us up as we effortlessly floated. We were told that you couldn't sink in the Dead Sea. Floating without any effort, well - you just don't forget something like that.

After driving back to Jerusalem, which is where we started from, we ended up at a lovely restaurant nestled in a park setting. My cousin called a friend of hers she hadn't seen in some time, who shortly thereafter showed up and joined us.

That woman told us that through a program called "Kindertransport," at five years of age, she was one of 10 thousand children who escaped German concentration camp fates, when her parents and other parents from Germany, Austria and Czechoslovakia put their children, if they chose to do so, on trains ending up at foster homes in England. The parents of those children – by doing that – didn't know if they would ever see their children again.

In all that my wife and I saw and experienced while in Israel, I can only say we were so fortunate to have seen, firsthand, what we had only read about in the Bible. Reading about it and actually seeing where it all happened, I can't stress enough, are two vastly different things.

Israel … truly holy ground.

Mind blowing.

Hope We Learn

January 20, 2010

On the last day of our recent Israeli tour, my wife and I visited the Holocaust Museum in Jerusalem, dedicated to the 6 million Jews killed in German concentration camps.

Of the two structures that comprised the museum, one was dedicated to 1 ½ million children alone, who were killed by the German killing machine. Upon entering it, on one wall, were about 18 or so pictures of children, each picture about three feet by three feet. Looking at those pictures and knowing the fates of those beautiful-looking children was heart-breaking.

We then walked single-file next to a rail you had to hold on to as you proceeded along because it was dark and all you could see was what appeared to be lit candles through a tall, translucent curtain. What you heard on the sound system was a female voice stating, concurrently in English, Hebrew and Yiddish, each name of the million and a half children, along with their age and where they were from. We learned that it would take one year for the list to be read from beginning to end.

In the second building, we saw a massive amount of evidence leading up to and including what took place in the concentration camps – dedicated death camps. It was almost too much to take in. For instance, one exhibit on the floor was a portion of the actual train tracks that delivered the innocent people in cattle cars to the concentration camps.

Another exhibit simply showed an approximate six feet by three feet pile of various sized colored shoes.

Shoes.

It was most sobering knowing the fate of those who wore them.

When walking out of that building, while trying to make sense of all the various exhibits and videos we had just witnessed, I stuttered to my wife, "Man's inhumanity to man. Evil at its vilest. It just doesn't make sense."

She replied, "So it will never happen again."

I had heard that statement so often over the years when the subject of the Holocaust was brought up, but at the moment my wife said that, it was as if I never heard it before put so clearly.

We visited the museum's bookstore where I browsed through some of the myriad of books dedicated to the Holocaust. I found one entitled, *I Escaped From Auschwitz*, briefly reading a small portion of the author's escape. I bought that book that told, in great detail, what went on at Auschwitz, the largest of all the German concentration camps. It told of the author Rudolf Vrba and his friend Alfred Wetzler's bold escape, the first successful one of its kind. They hid for over three days in the camp, in a hollowed out woodpile covered with wood planks, sprinkling gasoline on tobacco to confuse the German dogs from finding them.

They trekked by night to Slovakia, 80 miles in 11 days. That book is also known as *The Auschwitz Protocols* that led to the first realization of what was happening at Auschwitz told in great detail. For up to then, the world did not know, so secretive the Germans were in keeping it that way.

Those being transported to the concentration camps were told they were being "resettled" only to find, at the very last second, it was to their shocking end.

A moment in history still difficult to grasp, except to say – it must never happen again.

Look How Close We Are!

February 17, 2010

I was on a recent early morning flight from Syracuse to La Guardia Airport in New York City. I was alone and had a window seat. The plane was flying very, very low – about 10 minutes from La Guardia in New York – and I could see the panorama of city buildings of what I guessed to be New Jersey or perhaps New York City itself.

There wasn't a cloud in the sky.

I suddenly recognized what looked like the Chrysler Building and then, logically near it and above them all, the mighty Empire State Building. Looking toward the end of the island, there she was … the green lantern of hope for all entering the New York Harbor, the inspiring Statue of Liberty.

It was a thrill seeing all of that especially since we were flying so low.

I did a little sleuthing since.

The Bank of Manhattan, now 40 Wall Street, was newly completed and considered to be the tallest building in the land.

At the same time, New York's Chrysler Building was nearing completion. But, unbeknownst to the outside world, hidden inside, was the now recognized spire that, one week after the completion of the Bank of Manhattan, was put in place. The Bank of Manhattan had worn the "Tallest Building" title for a mere seven days.

But the race was far from over for, one year later, in 1931, the Empire State Building was completed, wearing the then new, undisputed Tallest Building in the World crown.

On a Saturday in July of 1945, a U.S. B25 Bomber crashed into its 79th floor, opening a 20-foot gash where 14 died.

There are a thousand businesses in the Empire State Building. It even has its own zip code. It's undergoing renovations to make it a more energy efficient and eco-friendly structure. Want to hazard a guess as to how much they're spending for that?

Try $120 million.

Just for renovations!

So, as I sat in that plane, looking at all below me as it flew over the Chrysler and Empire State buildings, and then over the Statue of Liberty, I thought if anyone was looking up – particularly in the Empire State Building area, essentially mid-Manhattan – they'd wonder why the plane I was on was flying so low.

The corners of the 61st floor of the Chrysler Building are graced by eagles, replicas of the 1929 Chrysler hood ornaments. On the 31st floor, the corner ornamentations are replicas of the 1929 Chrysler radiator caps. In 2005, New York's Skyscraper Museum chose the Chrysler Building as their #1 of 25 New York towers. Every time I see that magnificent spired top, it's a thrill.

Oh – do you want to see the Statue of Liberty any moment of the day live? Go to www.earthcam.com/usa/newyork/statueofliberty/.

It took nine years, working seven days a week, to complete building that inspiring statue.

As many of you know, currently the tallest building the world has ever seen is the Burj Khalifa in Dubai, United Arab Emirates. At the peak of construction, 12 thousand people worked daily on it. That's a lot of work shoes. Do the math.

Dubai, United Arab Emirates, let me see, I think you take a hard right at Poughkeepsie.

Seek and Ye Shall Find

April 14, 2010

My wife and I were seated in first row seats on the left side of the plane in the coach section. I sat on the aisle seat and in front of us was a wall, and on the other side of that wall, was the first class section.

As we sat there, a tall man walked by from behind me into the first class section.

He shortly, thereafter, returned, stopping next to my seat, talking to a man sitting in back of us … telling him how he wanted to stand and stretch a bit. They discussed the Boston Red Sox, seemingly knowing in depth the players they were talking about.

When that conversation seemed to end, I looked up at him and, knowing Syracuse was about to play Butler, asked, "What are your thoughts on the NCAA basketball tournament?

And, thus, I began a conversation with him that unfolded the following information:

He's 6'5" and graduated and played basketball in the '60s for LaSalle University in his hometown of Philadelphia. He averaged 24.1 points per game and was one of the top 20 scorers in the nation.

On his team was a fellow player Bill Raftery, the famous ESPN announcer, both of them friends to this day. They played against Syracuse, which had Jim Boeheim on its team, as well as one of the most celebrated SU players of all time, Dave Bing. When I asked him his opinion of Bing as a player, he said he was quick, had a great jump shot and referred to Bing's playing ability as, "Unbelievable."

Asking him about SU's current heralded basketball season, he said he watched Scoop Jardine, one of Syracuse's stars, play high school ball in Philadelphia where Jardine was from, commenting he was an outstanding player.

The man's name? Frank Corace, pronounced "chorus."

After college, a job in sales brought Frank to Utica to seek business from GE. He commented on the challenging winters in Utica. I told him Boonville's were worse.

He was the type of man that you read about in motivational books, being positive about anything we talked about.

I told him I'd send him a copy of the column if I wrote one about our conversation. He told me he'd forward it to Bill Raftery.

When my wife and I were walking down the tunnel on the way to our plane, I briefly spoke with another gentleman about SU and their chances in the NCAA tournament. He was from Hamilton, New York, and when our flight landed in Fort Myers, he suddenly reappeared. He told me how he was sitting near me and my wife and had overheard tidbits of the conversation with Frank. He was particularly impressed that he played on the same team as Bill Raftery against Jim Boeheim and Dave Bing.

That man told me his son graduated from Clarkson, and I informed him my daughter graduated from there as well.

Oh – last week I had lunch with my 6' 4 ½" oldest brother Michael and told him about meeting Frank Corace on the plane and how he played against Boeheim and Bing.

Michael then told me the story of how he played against Boeheim and Bing on a basketball team comprised of Utica All Stars and went up for a rebound against Bing, remarking, "All I saw was his belt buckle."

Rain, Rain – Enough Already!

April 28, 2010

A few observations about New York from the recent trip my daughter and I took to that incredible city.

It was predicted that New York was going to have heavy rains and winds during our stay there.

Those predicted rains started the Friday night we arrived. But it wasn't until the next day that we experienced its fury. On that Saturday morning, we were in a discount merchandise store, and I noticed, as we walked in, umbrellas for sale at $3.49.

My first thought, prophetic, was how could umbrellas that cheap be any good? At the checkout counter, I asked the cashier if the umbrellas I was buying could be any good at that price. Speaking in a heavy Spanish accent, I never did figure out what he said. That should have been a clue, but I bought two anyway. I think they call people like me fools.

As you know, there's a way to maneuver an umbrella so that you try not to let the wind get underneath it for, if the winds are strong enough – and the winds were all of that and more – the umbrella inverts most of the time, snapping the metal arms that previously held it up.

My daughter went through hers in about 20 minutes.

To go through mine, it took experienced me 14 seconds more.

My daughter told me that she had seen a broadcaster on the TV news earlier with a useless inverted umbrella, proving to the world watching him how strong the New York rain and winds were. And, although he didn't say as part of his newscast that his umbrella cost $3.49, we guessed it to be considerably more.

That afternoon, we went to the American Museum of Natural History where we saw, among other jaw-dropping exhibits, a stuffed whale the size of Pensacola. Unless you've seen it, you wouldn't believe it.

When we left the museum in the late afternoon, walking the short 150 or so yards to the subway entrance, as we battled the heaviest rains and winds I think I've ever experienced, we couldn't help but notice abandoned inverted umbrellas everywhere. It was like an umbrella cemetery.

While roaming the New York rain-soaked streets, we saw a Lexus taxi. I remarked to my daughter that earlier in my life when in Lisbon, Portugal, all the taxis there were Mercedes-Benzes.

When driving back home on the Thruway near New York, we drove over a rise and saw, in the oncoming lane, stopped traffic as far as the eye could see, with accompanying trooper cars with their lights flashing at the front of that seemingly endless line.

At first, we thought it was an accident, but then saw a huge puddle on that road's inside lane. A couple of vehicles had tried – one at a time – to plow through the puddle to the problem-free other lane. They didn't make it and were just sitting there … that's why the traffic was stopped. Because the lines were so long waiting their turn to get through, if I were in that traffic, hours I guessed, my family and friends would be visiting me in some mental institution.

At least once in a while.

You can only hope.

A Hundred Thousand – Dollars?

May 12, 2010

Last year when my wife and I spent some time in Bonita Springs, Florida, we'd pass a big Steinway Piano Gallery I wanted to visit, but we couldn't fit it in at the time.

This year, we went back to Bonita Springs and this time, I made it a priorty, visiting it.

My wife dropped me off one mid-morning while she shopped nearby.

On each piano was a three by five card with the model number and its price, along with some additional information describing it.

On one grand piano, the information on the card shook me.

It read it was Oscar Peterson's piano.

The price tag also read that piano was selling for 85 thousand dollars.

Familiar with his fame and some of his work as a jazz pianist, I sat down at that piano for a brief time and played on it to hear what it sounded like. It was one of those great, old, strong sounding pianos, but right or wrong, I was uncomfortable playing on it, allowing myself to feel intimidated by it knowing it was such a famous person's piano.

I've got to work on that.

I recall saying to myself, "I can't believe I'm playing on Oscar Peterson's piano."

Oscar made his United States debut in 1949 at Carnegie Hall in New York. His father, a porter for the Canadian Pacific Railway, would give his children musical assignments to do and when he returned from his weekly trips, he'd then go over their progress.

Oscar loved baseball but watched his sister, who practiced her piano diligently, copying her successfully to his dad's critical eye.

Drugs, notoriously prevalent around the jazz scene, had no impact on Oscar. In a February 21, 2003 interview by Bob Edwards for NPR's *Morning Edition* interview, Oscar commented on the drug scene, "I promised my mom I wouldn't get into any of this and if she were ever to hear any of this, it would kill her. And besides that, if I ever got busted down here in the United States, they'll never allow me to cross the border again. And between those two things it sort of got me through a lot of that."

Wise man.

A few pianos away from Oscar's was one owned by Billy Joel. His was a bit smaller and newer than Oscar's and was one of the most beautiful sounding pianos I've had the pleasure of playing. Just beautiful.

I've always loved his song, "Just the Way You Are." Some of those lyrics:

I said I love you, and that's forever
And this I promise from the heart
I could not love you any better
I love you just the way you are.

My father would have said price-wise about almost all of the pianos there, "They're not giving them away."

I played on one that cost $100,000. Would I buy one at that price were I to be in that financial bracket?

I'll let you know.

Freedom Land, Isn't That Near Jersey?

November 24, 2010

My cousin Elaine from Israel emailed me a few months ago that she and her husband were going to attend a folk music festival near Ellenville, New York, in the Catskills. And wouldn't it be a good idea if our family attended that festival so we could all meet up?

At the beginning of my junior year at Utica College, a folk music group was being formed by one of the students there. I went to where I was instructed several of that group were meeting, walked in to their student union and saw a girl and two guys sitting on the floor. The guys were playing guitars.

I had brought mine and quietly sat down next to them. One, Kurt Rolfes, was playing an instrument I had never seen before, a 12-string guitar. He and the girl, Lynn Jones, were singing a folk tune. Their voices meshed with a magnetism that was – enthralling.

I got brave on the next song and started singing with them. I then found out I was blessed with a gift of being able to harmonize and took the high harmony. And that's when it happened. The sound of the four of us, that included David Sumberg, an excellent guitar player, was as they say, "All she wrote."

A number of weeks later, encouraged by Kurt's incredible photograph of the group on posters throughout the college, a standing room only crowd of students filled their auditorium to hear the debut of what we named the group, "The Gallows Singers."

We received a standing ovation and rave reviews.

Several weeks later, we won an audition with others who had also won, as the backup talent for Oscar Brand, a well-known folk singer, songwriter and author. He was to perform at Syracuse's prestigious Landmark Theatre.

A limited release album was made of all the supporting talent who sang at that concert, the cover of which shows The Gallows Singers center stage with the other talent on each side of us, all singing a gospel song we suggested, "I'm On My Way."

Some months later, David Sumberg left the group and replacing him was Gene Rice, a most gifted Utica guitar player who sang bass. Gene would perform a guitar solo that combined "I Wish I Was in Dixie" and "The National Anthem" at the same time – a showstopper.

About a year later, we made an album recorded in New York entitled, "The Gallows Singers Swingin'", distrubuted by United Artists Records.

For two years, we sang mostly at colleges, as well as some clubs and private parties, and it was most exciting. When we sang, there was magic in the air.

When college graduation time came, the group split up.

At a Catskills hotel recently, at one of their folk music events, I briefly told The Gallows Singers' story and what a whirlwind experience it was. And how, from that time on, "It was all downhill."

I then sang with my guitar, Woodie Guthrie's classic, "This Land Is Your Land," and pretty much all there joined in. Just like the old days.

Oh – here's the main chorus to "I'm On My Way" we all sang and recorded, at that Syracuse concert:

I'm on my way, to freedom land,
I'm on my way, to freedom land.
I'm on my way, to freedom land,
I'm on my way, great God, I'm on my way."

I have to be honest with you; not that I've been lying to you up to now – but I can certainly wait until that happens.

R-L, David Sumberg, Kurt Rolfes, Lynn Jones and me in tree.
This was the picture posted around Utica College for
The Gallows Singers first performance. 1963

The Gallows Singers: (front to back): Me, Gene Rice, Kurt Rolfes
and Lynn Jones, 1963. This picture was on the back cover of
"The Gallows Singers Swingin'" album, 1964
(Both Gallows pictures were taken by Kurt Rolfes, who had a
photography scholarship to Utica College)

Is That Boonville Down There?

February 9, 2011

So the geese are all down south. Smart ... those geese.

We fight the cold and snow in the north country and the geese are where the warm winds blow. Moreover, not one of them isn't there because they can't afford a condo.

They seem to have a language that appears to be limited. But then again, who are we to know that? They could be talking to each other about the state of affairs as they "fly over".

"Oh, look Beatrice, there's that red barn down there we always pass over; its front door seems to be finally falling off. You think they would have fixed it by now. We'll talk later, gotta move up ... see you."

I wonder if, when they're on the ground, they talk to each other. Because they certainly don't have much time to do that when they're up there flying, each one moving methodically up to the front and then, when there, shortly thereafter, it's back to the back.

I also wonder if geese tell silly jokes to each other so one of them can justifiably say to the other, "You silly goose."

I wonder if there's such a thing as a serious goose.

Here's a possible conversation between a couple of geese, on the ground:

"Hey gander, how come you're always described as silly?"

"I'm glad you asked. It's a bad rap all of us geese have gotten over the years. I don't know who started it, but nobody takes us seriously. Silly they call us. You know what that does to you over time? I got to tell you I'm sick and tired of it."

"You don't look silly? I have an idea, why don't you get

together with some of your fellow "Ganderites", and, oh – put on a play, a serious one like, *Romeo and Juliet*. If that's too classical for your taste, consider a comedy, like *The Odd Couple*. Then people won't call you silly anymore because they now would see your vast talents.

"Don't be silly."

Tell me this then.

"What's that?"

The expression, "What's sauce for the goose is sauce for the gander."

"I've often wondered about that, what <u>does</u> that mean?"

Well, I guess, if it's all right with you, it's all right with me, something like that.

"Yeah, I've heard that but I still don't like it."

Why?

"It doesn't leave all of us geese out there, with some kind of positive – oh – message."

You're too sensitive. You think, for instance, dogs are all feeling down from the expression they "work like dogs?"

"Yeah, I don't think I like that but I'm not sure why."

I don't know. I haven't really seen too many dogs work hard; in fact, it's most common for them to sleep their entire lives away if you let them. I must admit though, they are known as, "Man's best friend."

"I'd rather have that than being called silly."

Listen, as you know, it's time to do some flying and honking, so take care of yourself and see you up there as we pass each other.

"Fine, catch you up above."

Don't forget that play idea.

"I was thinking, maybe I could write one."

What would you call it?

Geese Who Honk Together Stay Together.

His Height Got Me

April 4, 2012

On a recent, beautiful Florida vacation day – after settling in with our beach chairs mere feet from the water – my wife and I observed a young man fishing near us.

He was not catching any fish as he stood on the lip of the shoreline and waded further into the surf. He was up to his chest, casting from there. It didn't take long before he caught one and slowly walked back to the shore with the fish he had just hooked. It looked to be about eight inches long.

As my wife and I walked over to see what he had caught, a small group of mostly children had gathered, leading us to believe what he caught was out of the ordinary. The fisherman announced – holding the twisting fish by the tail – that it was a small hammerhead shark. He held it respectively away from the gawking children, remarking that the young shark's teeth were dangerous.

He told the children that if he didn't let it go, it would die.

The small group dispersed and the fisherman, shortly thereafter, picked up what we later realized was a circular net. Looking intently into the surf just before him, he walked with it slowly towards where we were. He'd stop, every so often, focusing on what was in the surf before him.

He was directly in front of us when he suddenly whirled his body and the net in a circle, similar to how a shot putter gets his momentum before throwing the shot put. After one complete whirl with the net fanning out about six feet, he hurled it into the surf.

Wasting no time, he immediately pulled the net out of the water that housed what looked like a goodly number of tiny twisting and writing minnow-like fish. Returning to his original fishing post, he emptied what he caught into a small container, such as you'd use to keep a six-pack of beer cold in. He then went back into the surf with that container floating beside him and proceeded to fish.

There's something about sitting on a beach – with the sun pouring down – that defines what a vacation is all about. Particularly knowing back home, it was winter.

On the way home, while waiting for our baggage at the Syracuse airport, I noticed an unusually tall, maybe 6'8", African-looking man. At first, I thought he was a basketball player, and approaching him, started a conversation.

We talked about Syracuse's great basketball season, and I asked if he played the game. He told me he didn't, never had, and lived in Syracuse for the past 10 years. I asked what he did, and he told me he was a motivational speaker who traveled the country, further mentioning one of his foundations built a hospital in Sudan. He introduced himself as John Dau.

We exchanged business cards, and it wasn't until two days before this column was due that I picked up his card, went to his website and found out what I'll tell you about in the next column.

I'll give you a hint. On his web site, a quote stood out at the top that said: "The John Dau Foundation" is fulfilling the dream of the former "Lost Boy" and genocide survivor John Dau to provide healthcare in the war torn region of South Sudan, building and sustaining medical clinics and training community health workers."

At our goodbyes, he said, "Keep in touch. God bless you."

I told him I would and emotionally responded, "God bless you!"

Another hint: On his website, he's pictured with President Clinton.

And all at the baggage claim area … you just never know.

A Spellbinding Story

April 24, 2012

In my last column, I mentioned I'd tell you more about John Dau. When my wife and I returned from a recent Florida vacation, I met John at the baggage claim area at the Syracuse airport.

The day my last column came out, which featured him and his story, I spoke with him on the phone for two hours. I told him it was his 6' 8" height that compelled me to approach him at the airport to discuss basketball.

He replied, "I don't even know how to throw a ball. I play a different game, to help people in South Sudan."

At the airport, he told me that a hospital was built by one of his foundations in his African homeland of South Sudan, where he had fled many years earlier from the civil war. And, that he travels all over the country as a motivational speaker for his non-profit organizations to help his harassed South Sudanese people.

On the phone, I asked him how many beds his hospital has. He told me it started with 13 and currently has 47.

He informed me there's a documentary about him produced by *National Geographic* and a book out by the same name, *God Grew Tired of Us*.

I acquired them both from the library. You can, too.

After viewing the DVD and seeing John's story dramatically unfold, I was flabbergasted.

In 1987, as the civil war of Sudan divided the north against the south, John, at age 12, in the dead of night, escaped from his African village in the south, as the Sudanese northern forces attacked.

He escaped to Ethiopia, staying there for four years at a refugee camp.

Civil war then broke out in Ethiopia, forcing his continued wandering for hundreds of miles to a refugee camp in Kenya, where at the age of 18, for the first time, he learned his ABC's.

It was during those wanderings in both of those refugee camps that John and his fellow "Lost Boys of Sudan," as they have since been called, survived near starvation, thirst, disease, raids by the North Sudanese forces, along with killer hyenas, vultures and lions. You can't believe a human being could go through so much and survive.

In 2001, he was among 3,800 young "Lost Boys" refugees who resettled in the United States and was one of 140 sent to Syracuse.

He worked 60 hours a week at three jobs while attending Syracuse's Onondaga Community College, and went on to graduate from Syracuse University's Maxwell School of Citizenship and Public Affairs.

By a series of incredible events, John received a letter, through the Red Cross, 15 years after he had resettled in Syracuse. The letter contained the phone number of the refugee camp where his two brothers, mother, father and two sisters lived.

Up to that point, he didn't know if his family was alive or not. John referred to the phone call that he made to his family at the refugee camp as one of the most exciting moments of his life.

In the documentary *God Grew Tired of Us*, it shows John – 17 years after having fled South Sudan – being reunited with his mother and sister at the Syracuse airport. It is an unbelievable scene. Get the DVD that shows it. It's absolutely mind-boggling.

John's dramatic story – of escaping from his South Sudan village, to life in the refugee camps, to traveling to Syracuse and having explained to him what a light is and how to turn it on and

off, to learning what a refrigerator and toilet are, to being introduced to foods in a supermarket he had never ever seen – you have
to to see it to believe it.

I urge you to contact your library and get John Dau's DVD
documentary, *God Grew Tired of Us*.

You will see why it won the Audience Award and Grand Jury
Prize at the 2006 Sundance Film Festival and why he travels in-
ternationally telling his story of the continuing plight of South
Sudan.

It's an honor just to be able to tell you about the incredible inspiring story of John Dau, an authentic human rights leader, a true
hero to his people, and an inspiration to all humanity.

Duhhhh ...

May 15, 2012

Arriving 20 minutes before the program began recently, I was fortunate to sit in the second row on the end. In the row in front of me – three seats over – sat Leonard Pitts, the Pulitzer Prize winning columnist. He was about to speak at Utica College.

He was sitting quietly with an occasional person briefly speaking to him. All I had to do was get up, walk the few steps over to him and say – see – that's where I came to a quandary, for I didn't know what to say to him.

If any of you have ever read any of his columns, this man is strong, this man is bold, this man goes where most don't in the literary pursuit of the truth. Right or wrong, I felt intimidated by his literary strength. That's why I didn't approach him.

What was I going to say to him that didn't sound as if I was patronizing him? I might have received from him, an, "Oh, isn't that nice?" were I to have said, "You and I have something in common most don't here. I write a column for a 160 year-old weekly, the *Boonville Herald*, about 35 miles north of here where I live."

In fact, when Leonard shortly thereafter gave his brilliant talk about race, an incendiary subject, presented with logic and grace, he mentioned at one point of his discourse, he didn't want to talk to people who just compliment him, preferring strong opinions and thoughts from the people he spoke with. When he said that, I breathed a sigh I didn't approach him.

What a gifted man. I had to mentally run to keep up with him.

He's something else, acquiring many literary prizes, written numerous books with a new one about to come out, winning the

Pulitzer – the Pulitzer!

Patronizing or not, Leonard Pitts is an incredible writer.

And maybe my life will fall short of my expectations, because I didn't go up to him and say, "Leonard, you inspire me, for after reading your columns, it shows what a first class mind can conceive and express."

Or, "I read you but I don't quite fully understand you. You're too above my head." Or, "Leonard, I have a suggestion for you." I can just see him lifting a defensive eye saying, "Oh?" It's at that point I could have slipped into a mental state of no return subsequently requiring constant vigilance, or somehow went on, saying, "Maybe you could consider toning down your literary rhetoric for people like me who can't fully intellectually keep up with you."

He could have then said, "Go back to school."

And at the end of his talk, he came off the dais, walking right by me. All I had to do was stick out my hand and he would have shaken it. I could have then boasted I shook hands with a Pulitzer Prize winning writer. In doing so, what would I have said to him? "Gee, Leonard, you were terrific, even though I was at least two mental steps in back of you a good portion of the time." So I kept my hand to my side as he passed me, not saying a word as others converged on him.

Maybe I should go back to school.

Advertising? Nah...

May 30, 2012

After Utica College, I was at my first job in New York City with a massive theatrical agency. I had been there for three years and was called in by the vice president of the company.

He told me he had to let me go because I wasn't putting enough of the talent the firm represented on TV shows. I had put many of the clients on those shows, but the company apparently felt it wasn't enough. I vividly recall him also complimenting me on my abilities, baffling me as to why, if that was the case, I was being fired.

As my life went, I then tried being a working actor in New York for five years. One obviously doesn't have the job whose auditions one goes for, so when I didn't get any of them, I wasn't technically fired for a role I never had, but it sure felt like it.

Moving to Los Angeles and opening my own theatrical agency, I didn't have to worry about being fired. What was I going to do, fire myself?

As the years evolved, I made it back to my home town of Utica, selling electronic typewriters. It was not an easy "sell" and my crowning achievement was selling – at one time – three of them to a hospital. It wasn't too much later that I was summoned to the boss's office, whereupon I was fired for generally not selling more.

I then entered radio, working for a couple of different stations, one of which fired me for a reason to this day, I have yet to figure out.

Two and a half weeks later, as a car salesman, I was fired for not selling enough vehicles. That I did understand.

Fourteen years ago I opened, with a partner, the advertising agency in Utica I continue to be a partner of.

After I closed my LA theatrical agency because I was not en-amored with the whole show biz scene, I reverted to typing to survive until my next serious life move.

I was engaged by UCLA's employment agency typing for various areas, one, at their psychological and counseling services department. I would register students who came in to take their interest and aptitude tests. After the students took the tests, they were then counseled by a staff of psychologists who interpreted the results for the students.

A perk for me working there was that I was able to take the test, which I did. The results told me that highest on the list was "music/drama/writing". It also showed I was in the top ten per-cent (interest and aptitude-wise) of advertising executives in the United States.

All that stood out from my top aptitude and interest test re-sults of "music/drama/writing", was 'drama', which I associated with - REJECTION - from all those auditions I took for so many years. So I immediately dismissed that option. Little did I envision where the other two parts, 'music' and 'writing' would years later take me.

Go figure.

You would have thought, since I was searching for life's next answer, I'd go to work for an advertising agency. It took me until years later to do that and only after being fired from a restaurant supply business that I worked at for seven years. And that was be-cause the owner was giving up that business and, instead, opting to open a supermarket.

Remembering years earlier the UCLA interest and aptitude test results, I decided to pursue working for a Utica advertising agency, which I did for a one person firm, building relationships with my clients. It was several years later that I opened my own advertising agency with a partner.

Philosopher Friedrich Nietzsche said, "What doesn't kill you makes you stronger."

From his lips to God's ears.

(I retired from Carpenter & Damsky Advertising in December of 2012)

The Boonville Years

Over the Heart, Huh...

January 23, 2002

Living in Boonville for these past 19 years as I have, you meet and see people who distinguish themselves. Now I know we're all equal and no one is any better than anyone else, but still, there are some who just seem to stand out among the rest.

When I was a member of the Boonville Chamber of Commerce a bunch of years ago, Ken Martin was asked to give a presentation for some little pins or similar 'little things' that the Chamber was considering giving out to new businesses. So Ken came and showed us some of the choices his business represented.

I had seen Ken mostly march in parades. It was generally known he was a high-ranking marine officer. His proud posture when marching was always something to see ... and still is.

So when he came that night to give his presentation, I was most interested to see him in action. Contrary to my expectation of him pulling off some kind of George S. Patton rapid-fire delivery, his presentation was very laid back.

I would see him as a spectator at our high school football games, and once saw him quarterback a bunch of locals in football at the local Boonville Park. Under his tutelage, his team "beat the pants" off the other team.

And then there was Dec. 8 of last year that I saw him unlike I had ever seen him before. It was at the Adirondack High School basketball game against visiting Herkimer, played here in Boonville, the day after observing Pearl Harbor Day.

Before the varsity game started, Adirondack's football coach, Dom Ventriquattro, introduced both teams as they stood facing each other in the middle of the gym. He then mentioned, with the color guard also present, how Ken Martin would say a few words.

The color guard came in and stood at the far end of the court at the foul line. They stood at rigid attention as Ken, with a hand-held mike, stood at the sideline at mid-court. And, in his full marine uniform, spoke first about Pearl Harbor. He pointed out two locals, one of whom was Harland J. Hennessey and how Harland had marched in the Bataan Death March in the Philippines. How, for 100 kilometers, none of those marching could have any water and those who fell by the wayside were shot ... and how Harland completed that death march and subsequently died in a prisoner of war camp from Beriberi. As most around these Boonville parts know, the local VFW is named after Harland.

Ken then asked how we'd feel if we ran up and down the basketball court – or ran anywhere – and weren't able to have water ... giving us some minute indication of what it must have been like in that Bataan Death March.

He also spoke of 9/11 and how all the students sitting in the gym should cherish the freedom they have ... because of the soldiers of Pearl Harbor who didn't make it, as well as the civilian 'soldiers' who died at Ground Zero ... all of them dying to save our freedom. And that because of Ground Zero, we were once again at war, yes, 60 years after Pearl Harbor.

Ken Martin was very eloquent when he told us how – when we're singing "The Star-Spangled Banner" – we should all take our hats off and put our hands over our hearts and think of those who died to give us the freedom to watch that Herkimer/ Adirondack basketball game.

When he was through speaking, Adirondack Senior Jenny Lee beautifully sang "The Star-Spangled Banner." While she sang, I noticed that most people had their hands over their hearts.

As the color guard marched out of the gym, Ken went over to

the Herkimer coach and shook his hand, wishing him luck. He did the same with our Adirondack coach, waving to the crowd as they clapped in appreciation for what he and the color guard had just done, walking out proudly to join them.

Ken Martin is a jewel.

Yes, indeed ... let freedom ring!

A Basketball Miracle

February 13, 2002

(Our Adirondack High School junior varsity basketball team had managed to win one game three-quarters of the way through the season. West Canada Valley beat us earlier in the season on their court by 41 points. This column is about when they came to play us on our court.)

Because West Canada had beaten us there by the numbing 41 points they did, when they came here to play us, we all tried forgetting that statistical sobering imbalance. Some would call it denial; I would prefer "blind faith."

And sure enough, West Canada controlled us during the first half, although we played with more life than any of the Adirondack parents, relatives, loyal fans and cheerleaders had seen all season.

When the first half ended, we were down by 10 points, and we all knew it could have been a lot worse. My son, Deane, had taken a number of shot attempts in that first half, but hadn't scored. I thought that was a good sign, for it meant that he was so much closer to scoring. Having sold typewriters, I hadn't sold any and I was told - because of that - I was so much closer to selling one.

In that West Canada basketball game, Adirondack was unrelenting in their defense, playing together as a team like none of us had seen them do all season. We were slowly and dramatically chipping away at West Canada's lead. There seemed to be a more than usual number of Adirondack fans present who were as vocally supportive as I've seen any of them ... perhaps because they saw in that effort, some hope in a season that was so mired in defeat. Seeing us gain on West Canada was like seeing a miracle before our very eyes; we weren't sure if it would disappear through our fingers like invisible sand.

The pace of the game was furious, and suddenly, there were but a few minutes left in the game. Adirondack had clawed back and was actually slightly ahead. Ahead! It was as if we were all "levitating", whatever that means ... hold on: "to rise or to float in the air, as if weightless." Yea, it sure seemed that way.

But West Canada came back at us and took the lead. Excitement in that gym was as feverish as I've ever seen it just about anywhere ... anytime ... galactic or beyond.

Then, suddenly, my son Deane took a three-pointer and made it! We were, once again, miraculously ahead. Oh my, the excitement!

Shortly thereafter, he took another three-pointer and made that one! It was emotional "outer limits" time. And, if that wasn't enough in that incredible drama, Deane made his third straight three-pointer! Total ... absolute ... unyielding ... chaos! It put us ahead by five points.

West Canada answered with a three of their own, coming back within two points. I recall inwardly pleading, "Please, dear God, let us win a game, this one!"

Adirondack's Jared Lee, who had kept us in the game with his consistent scoring, was fouled and made one shot that put us ahead by three.

And, miracle of all miracles, that's where the game ended. Not only did we win a game, we beat the team who earlier beat us by 41 points!

It was, unquestionably, the most exciting basketball game I had ever seen.

I told Deane, after the game, that he did what every player dreams of doing when they play basketball – making the shot or shots which, in his case, helped win the game. Now it wasn't that he did it alone, because he didn't. His teammates deserved equal credit, along with their coach, who led them with extraordinary inspiration. But most importantly, Adirondack played with a unified, dauntless and superb heart.

In close games, someone has to "step up." At that West Canada battle, destiny had it that it was Deane's turn.

Basketball.

Whew.

It showed everyone there, if you show up in life with an unrelenting heart and don't take no for an answer, that you can in fact slay Goliath just like David did – whether as an individual or a team.

What's That on My Chicken Soup?

September 24, 2002

It seems my son, Deane, a junior in high school, has shin splints. It manifests itself in his legs hurting him when he practices and races for his school's cross-country team.

In the discovery process, it came out that he's been practicing daily using his actual racing shoes. One "camp" says you're not supposed to do that, that those racing shoes are too light and you'll get shin splints. Further, they purport, if "one" practices with heavier running shoes and races with lighter ones, then he wouldn't have shin splints.

So his coach lent him what he called his "Rubber Ducky." It's one of those portable whirlpool contraptions that fits in the bathtub. The hope is that it will ease his shin splint problems.

The first night Deane tried it, my wife suggested I stick my head in the bathroom and see how he was doing.

As I opened the bathroom door, I was overwhelmed by the noise level the machine was making, coupled with the volume of the song Deane had on the radio in the background.

Both levels were so considerable that my, "How ya doing?" had to be hollered.

"What? I can't hear you!" he shouted back. I attempted it one more time with greater gusto.

This time, he heard me and laughingly said, "Fine."

My interpretation of his laughing was that it had something to do with old "Rubber Ducky" there.

Recognizing our communication problems, he told me he'd talk to me later. My response was to slam the door, signaling my acceptance to his suggestion.

About 10 minutes later, as my wife and I were watching Larry King on TV say good night to us and everyone else watching him, Deane came into our bedroom. I asked him how he liked the machine and did he feel it helped his legs.

He said he thought he liked it and remarked how only time would tell if it helped him. He then mentioned that the next time he used old "Ducky" there, or if on the off chance we had to use it, adding bubble bath would be a mistake.

Feeling more like a comedic straight man rather than a concerned father, I asked him, "Why?" He then pointed to his chest and remarked, with a chuckle, "The bubbles the machine kicked up reached unbelievable levels." I asked, as calmly as I could, if he had the shower curtain inside the bathtub. I was relieved at his affirmative answer … remarking how incisive of him to have done so.

So, another life altering lesson came across that night. Unless we want bubbles the size of Mount Vesuvius in our bathroom that could impact our entire house – in our case, those rooms underneath our bathroom that happen to be our kitchen and, below that, our cellar – well, we're going to hold off on the bubble thing.

By doing so, we wouldn't have to concern ourselves with opening our bathroom door and seeing a sight we never want to see. And, in the way our house is laid out, we wouldn't have to eat meals for probably years to come … with bubbles suddenly, mysteriously floating and landing on our spaghetti.

I guess the lesson is: don't use bubble bath. At least when we've got old "Rubber Ducky" charged up …

Bubbled broccoli?

Nah.

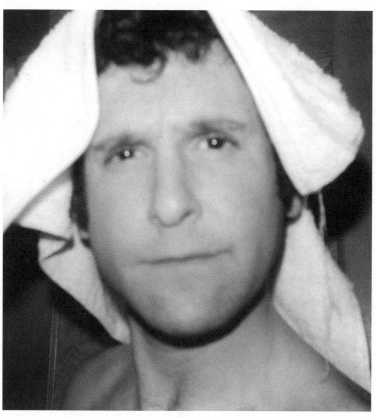

An uncanny resemblance to the Pharaoh

Say It Isn't So, Lady

December 17, 2002

Before going to a Christmas-related affair at Harts Hill Inn near Utica recently, my better half and I had to stop off at the J.C. Penney store at the mall in Utica. We were on schedule, but there wasn't much margin for error if we were to get to the affair on time. I parked my car at the entrance near the catalog section as my wife disappeared inside to take care of what she had to. I figured she'd be out in no time.

And chickens snowboard.

I sat in the car for an eternity. As impatience gripped me, I shut the car off and ducked into the store, glad to see my wife being waited on.

As I whisked past her, I told her I'd be right back. I went to the nearby fragrance section and went over to a cluster that caught my eye. I looked them over expediently because I had the car parked where it shouldn't have been. I found a choice I had never seen before, sniffing it lightly, knowing I had to make a quick decision.

It had a strange French name and didn't seem bad, so I applied it to my face. I then heard a female voice say, "Can I help you?"

It was a well-dressed, J.C. Penney sales lady. I told her I was all set. She said, "The men's colognes are over here," pointing to a slew of bottles where she was standing. I sheepishly said, "This isn't the men's section?" all too well knowing the answer. Too clearly, she responded, "That's correct."

With tremendous embarrassment, I power-walked back to where my wife was still being waited on. Passing her without missing a step, I whispered, "I'll be right back."

I entered the nearby men's room and tried washing the fragrance off my face, whose aroma by that time bordered on loathing. After vigorously wiping my face with liquid soap and brown paper towels, it gave my face a sort of red glow. Scrubbing a face with "many" brown paper towels will do that. Emerging from the men's room, my face beaming, I rushed past my wife who was miraculously still being waited on.

I returned to the scene of the fragrance debacle, fortunate that the sales lady wasn't around, and chose a men's – get that – men's fragrance I was sure of. As I hastily returned to where my wife was, I noticed that the massive amounts of brown paper towels didn't completely eliminate the original fragrance.

My guess was that a mysterious path would soon be cleared for me at the crowded Harts Hill everywhere I walked – all evening – because of the combined fragrances I had just applied.

Reaching my wife, who had just completed her marathon transaction, I was relieved as we walked out, that not only was the car still there, but there were no mall security with stern gazes to remind me of my errant parking choice.

Back in the car, as I told my wife the botched cologne story, she opened the window on her side – even though it was winter – to "let some air in."

The lesson:

Park where you're supposed to.

Haste makes waste.

You get nothing for nothing.

Carry your own soap, sandpaper and towel.

Nashville

February 5, 2003

It was in the late '70s. My friend Gene Rice was visiting Utica.
I sang and recorded with Gene years earlier back in my Utica
College days with, "The Gallows Singers." We decided to meet at
the Utica College pub in the afternoon.

While there, I sang and played a country song on the piano.
Gene then said, "What are you doing here in Utica?" intimating
that I should come to Nashville where he was a successful recording engineer.

Following my nose, I drove to Nashville in my car the following week – accompanied by everything I owned – to seek fame
and fortune as a country singer.

I lasted two weeks.

I ran out of money, typing jobs and musical hope.

I would sit and talk with a man who lived next to my motel,
while watching his vicious German Shepherd run back and forth
on a chain on a clothesline. The man proudly stated that, other
than himself, no human being had ever petted his dog. About the
second week, after having made eye contact with the dog for that
time, I got him to come over to me. As he wagged his tail, I petted
him. The man was flabbergasted.

I didn't include that on my resume. I probably should have for
all I was accomplishing.

Last week, I returned to Nashville to record two gospel songs
I wrote. At the recording session, before the drummer Gene
Chrisman left, I noticed, in script on the back of the coat he was
wearing, the words, "The Highwaymen."

I asked him what that meant. He told me that in the '90s he played drums on the musical tour with the Highwaymen that consisted of Kris Kristofferson, Johnny Cash, Willie Nelson and Waylon Jennings.

I then asked him who he recorded with over the years. He told me he was the drummer on the following recordings: Elvis Presley's "Suspicious Minds," "Kentucky Rain," and "In the Ghetto."

Can you imagine? If those recordings he played on weren't enough, my jaw dropped even closer to the floor when he then told me he also recorded on Neil Diamond's, "Holly Holy" and "Sweet Caroline," as well as on Aretha Franklin's, "You Make Me Feel Like A Natural Woman."

Unbelievable.

Of the three backup singers I had on that recording session, I asked Bobby Harden – the lone male singer of the three – which singer he had recorded with, who impressed him the most. He thought for a while, and then said, "Roy Orbison." I felt so privileged being privy to such credible insight.

So, now what to do with the two songs I recorded?

One is to get them played on any radio station that is willing to play that type of inspirational music. The second is to sing them live to the background music and voices. It also would help if I get some CDs made up of the songs. So I've got my homework cut out for me. And then, I'll just follow my nose. It's gotten me this far.

Nose, don't fail me now!

Sports History! We Saw It With Our Very Own Eyes!

April 16, 2003

They did it!

Now that the dust has settled a bit on all the excitement of Syracuse University winning the NCAA basketball tournament, I'd like to pass along some observations from that phenomenon.

I watched the game at a friend's house where we hooted and hollered as last week's final exciting game unfolded.

For those who didn't see the game, with less than a minute to go, with Kansas just three points behind, the television camera took a shot of Syracuse coach Jim Boeheim's wife, who was clutching their 4-year old son as only a mother can do when there's danger about. She had a look of grave concern – so near yet so far.

The excitement shortly thereafter peaked. With just seconds to go, Syracuse's Hakim Warrick sensationally blocked a Kansas shot, that had it been successful, would have tied the game forcing it into overtime.

And when the buzzer finally did go off and it was clear Syracuse had won, all Syracuse fans will probably remember that joy for the rest of their lives knowing it was Syracuse's moment of undisputed glory, for they were finally #1 in all the land – yes, national champions!

As much as it was a night of celebration for a team that deserved it, it was perhaps a vocational life triumph for their persevering coach Jim Boeheim. Up to last Monday night, he was considered a great coach by his successful statistics alone. Many reserved total greatness for him because he hadn't won the Big One, the one he won last week. He is now in the elite of all college basketball coaching legends. With last week's win, he has reached the pinnacle of his profession. And when he kissed his beautiful wife after the game, it was a poignant moment for all to see.

After the game ended, my friend remarked that it was too bad his father, a life-long Syracuse basketball fan, hadn't lived to see that momentous victory. I told him my father, also a devoted fan of the Orangemen, also missed that in his lifetime. For my friend and myself, Syracuse's historical victory will be unforgettable for that reason alone, because we did get to see it in ours.

Coach Jim Boeheim stuck to it for years and years and years, and kept building his wins inching up his success ladder. With last week's impressive triumph, he finally reached his mountaintop. He's a great lesson for all of us who have yet to reach ours. For if he can do it, so can we. It will take time as it did for him, with his 27 years as a coach, but hopefully we'll succeed with our dreams, as Jim Boeheim and his team did with theirs. We all know what our respective championships are.

Congratulations to Syracuse for accomplishing, what up to last week, was just an illusion. And I say to you who are "going for" whatever it is you've not yet attained - keep working hard at it as Syracuse did, as Jim Boeheim did, and you will end up with your dream coming true.

Don't ever give up. Ever.

Oh, that I live those very words.

Casabubu and the Turkey Thing

April 30, 2003

I ran into my friend Casabubu last week. I hadn't seen him in quite some time.

"Bah-ree!" he exclaimed. "What happened to your face, you crazy fool? Looks like one side of it slammed into something it wasn't supposed to."

"Well, Casabubu, you're not going to believe what happened. My wife was sitting in the passenger seat of our van, our teenage son was sitting behind her and I was driving. We were coming home after an Easter Sunday meal at my wife's side of the family. It was about 5 p.m. and I had the cruise control set exactly on 55."

"Sometin must have then happened … bad," Casabubu lamented.

I continued. "We were about ten minutes from Boonville on the main divided highway. I noticed a large turkey to my left, about the height of our vehicle, flying toward our car in a perpendicular direction."

"A turkey?" Casabubu gasped.

"Yes. We all remarked seeing it. I figured it would fly slightly over us or even behind us. But that didn't happen."

"What did?" Casabubu urged.

"It hit my driver's door window with a loud crash, spewing the shattered window in a shower of pieces that hit the three of us. I further felt a portion of the bird also hit the left side of my head before glancing off the top of the door frame. I may have blacked out for a split second, with feathers flying, and my sight blurred by all of that. It all happened so fast."

"Are you kidding me, this really happened?" Casabubu sincerely asked.

"I'm afraid so. The nurses, who later attended me at the St. Elizabeth Medical Center Emergency Room in Utica, remarked how fortunate I was that I hadn't lost control of the van. As I sat there on that gurney for the five and a half hours I was at the hospital, I gave thanks for the blessing that I wasn't hurt any worse than I was ... that my wife, who was X-rayed as well, was all right, and, of course, that my son was ok."

"Bah-ree, I can't believe that a turkey caused all that trouble."

"One of the two who took my X-rays at the hospital said he never heard of such a thing."

"So you'll be all right?" Casabubu asked. "Those bruises and cuts on your face that look like the bad guys in a western movie did you in - will they go away?"

"Yes, I'm told that."

"One last question I gotta ask you Bah-ree, before I go."

"What's that, Bu?"

"Tink you'll ever eat another turkey sandwich again?"

I thought for a while and then said, "I'm not sure." A woman at the hospital who heard my story remarked to her husband, "From now on, for Thanksgiving, we're having pork roast. Pigs don't fly."

"Bah-ree, take care. You're fortunate it wasn't worse than what actually happened."

I responded, "I think that's the lesson here. Appreciate what you have, because you just don't know."

"Bah-ree," he continued, "I love you, but you're still ah crazy fool."

Duck? Under What?

May 28, 2003

When working for the local radio station in Boonville in the '80s, it was common for me to go to Utica to sell advertising time to the car dealers, as long as I was back by three in the afternoon to do my radio show. I also had an official looking press card that I rarely used, but it made me feel so important when I did.

One morning, I had read in the Utica paper that an inmate from one of the local jails had escaped while being transported by van. That particular day, I went down to Utica to see my usual car dealer accounts. The afternoon found me driving back to Boonville on Route 12, a four-lane, fairly straight highway with a median.

A police car suddenly passed me going as fast as they love to go when it appears they have a mission. Shortly thereafter, a couple more went whizzing by. Suddenly, it was like an armada passing me, all with revolving red lights, going very, very fast.

Looking in my rear view mirror, I saw a sight I had never seen before or since, a continuous line of red-light-blinking enforcement cars as far as the eye could see. I never knew that there were so many enforcement agencies in the entire universe.

Then, suddenly, they all pulled over and parked in the center median. I decided to do the same, to, hopefully, "get the scoop" for my radio show I would be on in a short time. After parking in the median amidst all those official and intimidating cars, I approached the nearest policeman and, holding up my WBRV radio press card, asked him what was going on.

He said the prisoner who had escaped that morning from the

van in Utica was suspected of being in the barn he pointed to about 500 yards from where we were. I was a part of an exciting drama! Suddenly, they all jerked down as if a bullet had been fired in our direction. I heard nothing, but I too jerked down, soberly asking myself – not in a kind way – was I completely out of my mind for being there?

And then, in a manner of a few seconds – as if someone unplugged a giant bathtub full of police cars and their armed drivers – they all got in their respective enforcement vehicles and sped off back where they had all come from.

I continued driving back to Boonville, dumbfounded with what I had just experienced.

About four miles later, I saw a solitary police car parked on the right side of the road with a young-looking man leaning against the police car with his hands over his head and his back to that lone police officer who was holding a gun on him.

What was most unusual, I thought, was that the guy with his hands on his head was only clothed in his underpants. I kid you not.

Sleuth that I was, I figured he was the guy every police car in the galaxy I had just seen, was after, only in the wrong direction. Figuring I'd tell my listeners about it, since it was getting close to three o'clock for my show, I didn't stop.

When I shortly thereafter went on the air, I excitedly told my audience about what I had just experienced.

Did I consider heroic police work after that as an alternate career consideration?

"No" is not succinct enough.

My radio days at WBRV-AM in Boonville, New York,
with daughter Melissa, 1983

Fried Clams Heaven

July 23, 2003

Running into Casabubu recently, I couldn't wait to tell him of our family's approaching annual Maine vacation.

He patiently listened and said, "So Bah-ree, what's such ah big deal 'bout Maine?"

I breathed deeply and said, "Well, for one thing, the ocean. That ocean is ... so inspiring. To stand in front of it and just look at it is an experience that is difficult to put into words."

"I can see that," he said. "But Bah-ree, dot ocean of yours for swimming, I hear is colder than ah Boonville winter."

"Well," I proceeded to tell him. "I wouldn't go so far as to say that. Yes, it's a tad chilly, but ..."

Casabubu interrupted.

"Chilly? I hear it's very difficult to swim in. Ain't dot dee truth?"

"It has its temperature-swimming challenges," I admitted. "But even though it's not as tropically warm as your Caribbean Sea where you come from, it doesn't matter, for to be near it is an experience I reflect upon throughout the entire year.

"Bah-ree, my ocean where I come from, we swim in it, we dance in it, we roll around in it and the blueness of it is so beautiful."

I told him his ocean sounded just great and further remarked, "I guess we both love our respective oceans. I can't wait to see 'mine' up there in Maine. It has such a dramatic beauty and charm that makes it, in its own way, as beautiful as yours."

'Bah-ree," he continued, "What else does Maine have besides this ocean of yours?"

I responded, "Gray houses."

He hesitated for a moment and with a look of confusion asked, "Whuh-chu mean – gray houses?"

Enthusiastically, I blurted, "Casabubu, you've got to see them to believe it. They have houses painted gray, each one different from the next, that are so unlike the gray houses you see back here."

He tilted his head to one side and gasped, "You better go chase after your brain, 'cause it got away! Ah gray house is ah gray house ... in Maine or in Boonville!"

Undeterred, I plunged ahead, "Casabubu, I take a different view. Knowing you've never been to Maine, like I said, you've got to see those gray houses to fully appreciate them."

"Watta bowt dee food der?" he asked. "Well," I replied. "I wait all year to eat their clams and their lobster. For instance, the fried clams are so different from what you get around here. They're so big and tasty, it's "clam heaven.""

He responded, "I hear dee clam and lobster prices are higher than ah kite."

"Well," I said. "You just save up your pennies just like you would for any vacation."

"Bah-ree, tell me one more thing before I go. When you're up der in Maine, do you do any writing?"

I told him that I get up very early every morning, weather permitting, of course, and sit on one of those light metal folding chairs on the sand just feet from the breathtaking ocean, writing on my laptop computer. And, that writing like that is like a dream come true ... and that those are some of the greatest moments of all the vacation.

As he walked away and waved, he shouted, "Bah-ree, you still crazier than a cockeyed monkey."

I gotta tell you, when they made Casabubu, they broke the mold.

Where Did She Say?

November 26, 2003

I was given strict instructions by my better half last Wednesday to vote for our local school renovation project. Not to tell you how I voted, but here's a clue. If I voted a certain way and the project passed – after construction was completed – I'd never have to worry again about driving into the high school driveway in the winter … and my car and me falling into a pothole the size of Kalamazoo. Get my voting drift?

Since my wife voted earlier in the day and had to go to Utica that night – when we normally would have voted together – I found a note from her when I got home reminding me to vote and up to what time to do it. Earlier in the day, I thought she had said to vote at the same place at the school we always did. The last time I voted at the school, I seem to remember it was at the high school cafeteria, or something like that.

I drove up to the high school and approached the doors you'd go through to get to the cafeteria. They were locked – not a good sign. So I returned home, figuring I'd take a closer look at the note my wife left me that would tell me precisely where to vote, knowing it wasn't at the high school cafeteria. Sure enough, back home, there were the instructions I should have seen the first time. Voting was at the middle school, not the high school.

Charging down the street to what I thought was the middle school, I approached the doors bordering where I parked. The sign on the doors said "Enter the doors around the side of the building." I went to those doors and as my friend Casabubu would have said, "They were locked … tighter than ah clam."

"Middle school," I said to myself. "This must not be the middle school," passionately adding, "Ya bloke!"

I then deduced that the middle school was the building attached to the high school I went to the first time. High ... middle ... elementary ... all very confusing.

Undaunted, I drove back to the high school, this time to its attached neighbor, the middle school, whose front doors were unlit and desolate.

Painfully recognizing this was my last chance, I drove around the side of the building to the back, figuring that's where I'd find the elusive doors leading to where I should vote, knowing if they weren't there, when home, start packing my bags.

As I approached what I hoped and I might add – prayed – were the right doors, I was thrilled to see a lighted section. Election life!

When I arrived at those doors, I more than hoped were those of the middle school, there was a sign on them ... something about "Posted, Voting and 500 feet," signaling I had finally arrived at the right place.

Once in the voting room, I signed in. As I approached the voting booth, a retired male teacher I recognized was sitting next to it, with a woman sitting next to him. I spoke to him briefly and when I exited the voting booth after staking my voting claim, I said to the both of them, "I probably shouldn't tell you this," and then proceeded to inform them of my frustrating tale of voter building confusion. I ended my conversation by telling them I didn't think it was prudent telling my wife the story.

When home, after getting out of my car in the garage, I yelled out to no one, a passionate and frustrated, "I DID MY CIVIC DUTY!"

Just before my wife reads this latest tale, I'm going to go down in the cellar – with a blanket.

He Called You (gulp) - What Time?

December 10, 2003

When working in Boonville radio in the '80s, one of my primary duties was to solicit businesses to advertise on the station.

I'd then go on the air in the afternoon, which I truly enjoyed. For the years I did that, that unseen audience was like a collective friend I felt very close to.

On the air, I would play country music and, generally, carry on as much as I could. "As much as I could" meaning: whatever radio creativity inspired me at the moment. Another way of putting that is … whatever I could get away with.

One idea was having Boonville's first annual "Ugliest Dog Contest." I decided to hold it in the middle of our town park.

I plugged the contest on my radio show and sure enough, about six dogs were entered. There were some beauties. Maybe that's not exactly the correct word to use. One scrawny one was the undisputed winner. I don't recall what the prize was, possibly a box of Kleenex. By the way, that "annual" contest never made it to its resounding successful second year, or for that matter, any succeeding year.

But creativity hath no boundaries. I subsequently came up with another contest, this time a musical one.

I called it the "Wizard of the Week" contest. I would tell those listening to my show that, on the Friday of that week, I'd play a song and whoever called in and correctly named its title, would – for one week – officially be WBRV's "Wizard of the Week." They would also receive a coveted prize.

I went to nearby Rome to a T-shirt business and the deal was that, in exchange for mentions of that business, I'd give away a T-shirt a week emblazoned on the back with, "WBRV's Wizard of the Week."

The first week leading up to the contest was most exciting, and I liberally plugged it on my shows. Finally, that Friday arrived and it was show-and-tell time. I played a recently released country song I had played throughout the week on my show, and the first four or five callers incorrectly guessed its title. A male voice then called and, thankfully, answered it.

I was also on the air on Saturday mornings from 9 to noon, and it was common for my boss to come into the studio on that day. Sure enough, after the first time I held the wizard contest, there he was the next day.

While on the air, between songs, he nonchalantly asked me if I knew of a contest called, "Wizard something?"

Sensing trouble, I choked that I did, and as tactfully as I could, told him the precise name of the contest.

He went on to state that at about ten thirty the previous evening, while sleeping, he was unexpectedly awakened by a phone call. Seems the late night caller was the newly acclaimed "Wizard of the Week" calling from one of the local "watering holes", and the Wizard's friend who had not heard the show, didn't believe the Wizard had indeed won.

So, in an effort to persuade him, the Wizard called my boss and put his friend on the phone to get the true scoop. When my boss told me that, my brain took an unscheduled, unconsious skip.

Did WBRV's "Wizard of the Week" contest have great lasting power after that?

In the interest of full disclosure, aahhhh … not yes.

Interviewing Santa with him taking an order on the phone, 1986

My Son, the Jumbo - Headed Juggler

February 25, 2004

It's been awhile, but, at one time, I could juggle a couple of tennis balls or fruit with one hand. Not for very long … maybe 7 seconds. I knew I could get better if I kept practicing.

Now I'm not asking for any juggling accolades, for, even though it was a start, it was certainly nothing compared to people we've seen who can really juggle. Like with two hands. And more than just tennis balls or fruit. I would have liked to have graduated to eggs, but … well … we needed them for breakfast.

So why do I mention such a menial thing as juggling seven seconds with, say, two tennis balls in one hand?

I'll tell you.

I just read in the *Syracuse Post-Standard* that juggling "bulks-up" the brain." They did a study on it. Scouts' honor.

Seems some German scientists took brain scans of people, who, for three months, learned to juggle three balls for 60 seconds.

They found that the brain tissue of whoever did that success-fully … increased.

The brain grew.

And when they stopped juggling, expansion of their brain decreased.

So juggling can grow your brain. And, if you stop doing that, it goes the other way. I suppose the answer is, once you start, don't ever stop.

Let's see now. I'll find a juggling school … there's got to be one.

And I'll pack a bag … and go learn to juggle.

And I'll work my way up to juggling three balls for 60

seconds. To grow my brain, it will be worth the time away from my family and our one fish.

I'll definitely come home with a bigger brain than when I left. This is a good thing.

I think.

And when I come home from that school, I hope my family recognizes me. I'll probably have a bigger head. I presume, when you have a bigger brain, your head has to grow bigger to accommodate the growth. When I get home, I hope I'll be able to get through the door.

But, I'll do it right. Instead of going to school for three months, I'll go for a year and really grow my brain ... big time. After a year of juggling, I hope I can keep my head up and not flop over because I learned so well.

I'll be so smart.

Maybe I'll then open up a school myself. I'll call it ... "Boonville Juggling University". I can see it now on sweatshirts, BJU. I'll give out certificates and have graduation exercises every three months. I'll even be the graduation speaker and tell my students what juggling did for my life, uhhhh ... head.

If I can hold it up.

Another possible name choice for the school - how about ... "Bigger Head University", BHU? Maybe they'll call it what sounds like ... BOO.

"Where do you go to school?"

I go to BHU U.

Somebody will probably mistake it for a ghost school.

All of these decisions to make ... it reels the brain. I'm going to go juggle some tennis balls. I can't get in any trouble with them. My brain will start growing immediately and who knows where it will take me?

Hmmm ... BHU U. It does have a nice ring to it.

Shocked

June, 2, 2004

I was brought up on Kemble Street in Utica in a three-story yellow brick house my grandfather owned. That address was 1444 Kemble St.

My grandparents on my mother's side, and my oldest brother Michael lived on the bottom floor.

On the middle floor lived Mr. Smith and his housekeeper, Miss Body … quiet, unassuming … lovely people. He had an old car he never drove that occupied one side of the backyard two-stalled garage.

On the top floor, the address was 1446 Kemble St., where my parents, older brother Alan and I lived.

We ate breakfast on the third floor and lunch and supper at my grandparent's on the first floor. That's how we grew up. Up and down those back stairs a million times.

The neighborhood, like all neighborhoods, has changed over the years. On the front page of the Utica *Observer-Dispatch* this past April 2nd, I couldn't help but notice an article with a headline that read: **13 escape burning Kemble St. house**.

It got my attention.

The first paragraph told of 13 people avoiding injury in a Utica fire.

The second paragraph said, "At 12:45 a.m. firefighters responded to a fire call at 1444 Kemble St."

My mind did a mental snap.

The story went on to say how everybody got out of the fire, some through windows, and that the cause was unknown.

I emailed the story to my brothers and cousins.

Michael and I recently had lunch, the first time we saw each other since his recent lengthy stay in Florida. When I mentioned the Kemble Street fire to him, he was shocked. When I told him I had emailed him about it, he said he hadn't received it.

After lunch, we drove together to Kemble Street, and as we approached "it", I told him not to be shocked as to what we both might find.

When we got there, one word could best describe what we found – rubble.

Where once stood a proud, three-storied brick house, now was nothing more than just a burnt pile.

We walked around to the back where we guessed the fire started because the black scars were the darkest. We talked of how Mr. Smith and Miss Body had to endure our make-shift basketball games in our third floor kitchen as the three of us brothers played against each other, fiercely, as brothers do. Michael mentioned that when the basketball games got too hot and heavy, Mr. Smith would call downstairs and Grandpa would come up and yell at us.

I thought of taking a brick from the rubble.

But I didn't.

Days later, I was considering returning and getting one, when Michael called telling me he went back and retrieved bricks for us.

I visited Michael and his wife at their house after that, and he told me he'd give me a brick before I left. He had an appointment to go to, and I stayed and continued visiting with his wife.

When I left their house and approached my car, in front of it, standing on one end, was my yellow brick. Memories kicked in of what the house used to look like.

Any of you whose early houses are still standing, I suggest

you take a picture of it.

I didn't, but every time I see that yellow brick in our garage, it brings back memories.

Sentimental fool that I am.

My mother and father, circa 1930
(Notice the bricks)

Me, about 4

Kiss a What?

July 14, 2004

Our church is always thinking of new and innovative ways to raise money to pay its expenses. That's what churches do. Ours is no different.

When I first heard about it, I didn't quite understand it ... but, I recall I smiled.

I was one of five asked to give myself up if I won, to do what I think I heard you had to do if you won. I figured if it was for the good of the church, how could I say no? After accepting, I was told to pose for the camera and give my best pucker look. You know pucker – like when you kiss or get kissed.

As I was told to "Pucker well for the camera," something in me said I should have asked more questions.

Although I've never been asked for a pucker picture, my instinct said to myself, "Easy on the pucker, Bub."

For the next bunch of weeks at the Sunday morning services, Charlene Ludwikowski would tell the congregation the latest tally as to who was leading in the voting.

In the church hallway, lined up on a table, were five canisters, each one featuring a picture of the contenders. I was one of those five, the only one incidentally, with a limpid smile on my face.

The object was for the congregation to donate to which of the five they would like to see win. "Win" meaning whoever had the most money donated in his canister.

The winner – our very own pastor (bless his heart!) – got to do the following. After the second of three church services, around eleven twenty on a recent Sunday morning, he got to kiss ... a small pig. A live one.

I don't know if you've ever been around a small pig. I hadn't. It wore a leather harness such as you see dogs wear that – sort of – contained him. Charlene was holding on to him for dear life. A respectable portion of the three Sunday morning services stood in front of the church. They watched the little pig squeal, snort, buck and generally thrash about.

Pastor Bill Mudge, our valiant winner, stood just to the side of wherever the pig decided he wanted to go. I suspected Bill was trying to figure out how he was going to do what we all couldn't believe he was going to do.

And then, it finally happened. Bill kissed his right hand for all to see and, with that kissed hand, patted the pig on his head.

Bill's no fool.

We all breathed a sigh of relief and clapped vigorously.

When they backed up the pickup truck with young Porky's cage on it, a couple of guys lifted it down to the ground. They tried to get the pig back in his cage, but not before it put up a most respectable fight, snorting and squealing with considerable fervor. It gave me time to retreat some respectable distance from the action. After several attempts, they finally got the pig in the cage and clasped the door. We were all relieved, particularly our pastor.

I don't know how much money we made on the contest, and believe me, my ego was not bruised because I lost to Bill.

During the contest, I was considering taking out a second mortgage on my house, and depositing that money in – well, I won't say whose container – but I will tell you, it wouldn't have been mine.

If Elected I'll ...

October 19, 2004

Soon, the presidential election will be here. As usual, both sides are battling each other, and as you can see, not delicately.

Politics.

Something else.

The first elective experience I had was in high school, losing to my cousin when my fraternity voted him in as secretary and not me. I didn't have much time to wallow in defeat as I was then nominated and then elected to the post of treasurer. I'm not sure anyone ran against me, thus sparing me a second stinging defeat. The first check I wrote, as the fraternity's erstwhile treasurer, was returned. Two reasons: I forgot to put the date on it, and I forgot to sign it. It seems detail-wise, I was a bit unconscious. Fortunately, I got better. Worse I couldn't get.

Let's see now, politics huh ...

If I were President of the United States:

"Oh President Demsey, your tea is ready."

Ready for what?

"Next on your agenda, Mr. President, the ambassador from Zood-Zood is awaiting your presence in the Pump Room."

Zood-Zood?

"Yes, sir."

Do I have to see him?

"Yes, you do, Mr. President."

What's he want?

"For the United States to co-sign for a 185 billion dollar loan."

For what?

"I would have assumed you knew."

Gosh, he said something to me about that. Tell him, let's see, tell him … ahhhh … to go "pound salt". No, no, don't tell him that. Tell him I'm still studying it and when he's back the next time from Zood-Zood, we'll set up a meeting. Who's next?

"There's a Mr. Krapes Soozett from France who wants to meet with you, so he can give you a gift of some of his company's latest crop of wine France apparently is quite famous for."

Wine? It's 9:30 in the morning. Who wants wine? Tell him to leave it and we'll be in touch. Oh, and tell him thanks. Are there any other appointments?

"Yes."

Who?

"There are 700 Hawaiian dancers on the south lawn waiting to perform for you."

Perform what?

"What they refer to as their 'Dance of the Pineapples'."

Well, I guess I better go see them. Do we get any pineapples out of it?

"Yes, Mr. President."

How many?

"Fifteen tractor-trailer loads."

So as you can see, I wouldn't make a very good politician. Have I ever harbored any other elective offices other than the Presidency?

Well … maybe one more.

"Senator Demsey, what's your take on the new proposed tax on candy?"

I don't like it.

"Why?"

Candy's good and taxes are bad.

"Isn't that a little simplistic? Wouldn't you agree that without taxes, our society wouldn't be able to exist?"

You asked me.

"Well, Senator, we'll see how the voters take to that come this Election Day. Aren't you the least bit concerned your opposition will claim imminent victory because, what you refer to as your supposed honesty and candor, they call your severe lack of knowledge on the true issues."

Sticks and stones ...

"Senator Demsey, with the election upon us, what is your response that you're lazy? Senator Demsey – oh Senator Demsey! Would someone please wake Senator Demsey?"

The Umbrella Massacre

December 22, 2004

Recently, I bought my wife a Christmas present which is usually no big deal. But on that day, oddly for winter, it didn't just rain, it was a rain rampage.

As the sales lady went to gift wrap it, I had to go back to the car where I had left a coupon that could only be applied to the gift that day. While there, I checked my cellphone, which showed I had missed a call from a friend in Boonville, asking if I'd stop off at Walmart and purchase an item he needed the next day.

After completing the purchase for my wife, I drove relentlessly through the pounding rain to Walmart. When there, I took the umbrella I had in the car – one of those stubby 12-inch types, and when outside, I had a struggle to open it. When I finally did get it to open, it didn't stay that way, but instead started closing. To prevent that, I had to hold it at the top from the inside. Even though I had to use it in that awkward way, I was glad I had it, as the rain was seemingly reaching Noah-and-his-Ark proportions.

Returning to the car, I once again had to hold the broken umbrella from the top on the inside. When in the car, I threw it down on the passenger floor with frustrated passion, committed to eliminating it from my life at my earliest convenience.

Pulling into our garage at home and glancing down at the umbrella, I decided to throw it in the garbage can located in front of where I park my car. When I leaned over and picked it up in the car, it must have sensed its imminent demise, for taking me by surprise, it suddenly started to open. As it was filling my side of the car with its expansiveness, I was fighting to have it go back to its old deflated way.

The more I fought it, the more it opened, with water it still retained from the Walmart excursion spraying in all directions. But the battle was on and I was losing, getting swamped in the process. A beaten man, I "threw in the towel" by hastily opening the door to escape.

My commitment to ending the umbrella's life in the garbage was at a feverish pitch. Realizing I still had to get from the garage to the house, I spared its life one last time.

Holding it in the now all-too-familiar top fashion from the inside with my right hand, I proceeded to run the short distance to the house. When inside, my daughter, just home from college on her Christmas break, was a willing listener to the umbrella debacle I had just experienced.

I finished the story heroically declaring, "I'm going to throw it in the garbage!"

She had the umbrella in her hand and quietly informed me that it was indeed in proper working order, pointing out the button housed on the lower side of the handle. She patiently explained that if that button was pushed, the umbrella automatically opened. She further told me that, under those conditions, it would close correctly with no fight.

As I looked at her and then at the umbrella, feeling trapped, I searched my vocabulary for just the right word or phrase that would best describe how I felt.

I muttered, "Uhhhh ....button - shmutten"

What Bothers Me

May 4, 2004

What I'm not thrilled about:

The noise of vacuum cleaners. It makes me want to check in somewhere ... and I'm not talking about a hotel.

Anchovies. I tried them once.

Mosquitoes. May they all be banished to an island by themselves – far, far away.

Flies. I saw a film on them back in my Army Basic Training days that showed how many germs they carry. Had you seen it, you wouldn't like them either.

Colds.

Crying babies at restaurants.

Flat tires. I don't get them anymore, but I haven't forgotten when I used to.

Sunburns. That sun block stuff fortunately ends all that. But something always gets missed, like the tip of an ear or a spot on the chest.

Hot peppers. Once at Syracuse in my high school days, I put those brown hot kernels I didn't know were hot, on a piece of pizza and ended up shoving napkins in my mouth.

Thunder and lightning. Still scares me.

Dogs that yap. Can't tell you what I'd like to do to them.

Dogs that bite. Can tell you, but I'm not going to.

Cigarette smoke.

Strife.

Hiccups. My grandmother used to say, "Someone is thinking of you."

Condescension. If I were a judge, it'd be life for every one of them.

Toothpicks that break. What a scam.

Smoke from vehicle tailpipes. I used to be more verbal against them until one of my cars did it.

The smell of ammonia. I gag thinking about it.

Limp shower heads.

Guilt.

Swearing.

Snakes. The lowest.

Whiskey. That crazy I'm not.

Cuts while shaving.

Sauerkraut.

Dirty cars.

Bugs. Some look positively evil.

Spiders. My wife is worse than me. I have no trouble rescuing her from one when emotionally summoned, although I do have to yell at the moment of impact.

High pressure sales people. "No thanks." I said, "No thanks!"

Cold coffee.

Have you ever been "dropped on" by a bird? The opposite of thrilling. I was in Pamplona, Spain, at the "Running of the Bulls" during one of my summer college years. I was napping with a wide brimmed toreador hat over my head in the village square on one of those circular concrete benches around a fountain. I heard several splats on my hat that woke me. Several. What you think it was, it was. To this day I haven't been able to figure out … the "several" aspect.

From that incident, I've been reluctant to snooz in public.

At least outside.

Fatherly Pride

May 18, 2005

It just sort of whirred by. One day out of one's life – a couple of Sundays ago.

Momentous.

Taking a shower in a strange place in itself is unique, this one, at my daughter's apartment. I put the handle all the way to the end and waited for the hot water to come. And waited ... and waited. My wife happened to come in and rescued me from my frustration. She put the handle half way. It worked! Why didn't I think of that?

Everyone scurrying around ... eating breakfast while watching the Ray Charles movie we rented the previous evening. His first child seemed to be pretty cool. I asked what he did. Nobody knew.

A half hour to go ... whoa ... better get moving.

Good thing we got there early. All those people trying to get good seats. "Look, down there on the bottom, one row up from the floor, seats enough for all of us. Grab them!"

Got them. Whew.

The wait. Interesting looking people walking back and forth, interesting clothes, adorable children.

One fashionably dressed woman who looked to be in her forties threw her arms dramatically around what could have been her father, kissed him and then led him arm-in-arm to where she was sitting. To keep her hair out of her eyes, she kept sporadically throwing her head from side-to-side. All that energy just doing that.

The sound of bagpipers marching in signaled the beginning of the ceremony. I almost started crying listening to their dramatic sound. How many of them? Including the bagpipers, drummers, the leader, I counted what looked like 15 in all. What you do with your time ...

The ceremony was held in their hockey rink. The flags of those they played against hung high above from the rafters for all to see. Among the many were Cornell, Colgate, Harvard and Yale. I've seen some of those campuses. My goodness, some heavy hitters.

One honoree who spoke was a fluid mechanics scholar and educator, another an award-winning author, and the last, a pioneering environmental conservationist. All – if there is such a thing – beyond brilliant.

Since it was Mother's Day, the president of the college asked that all the mothers stand up. Wasn't that nice? What's that? He wants us fathers to do the same? That means me ... my goodness. Thanks.

At that moment, as they clapped, I felt so important standing among all the other fathers ... in whatever way we were responsible for our children's graduation ...

And then, one by one, the 600 plus graduates received their diplomas as their names were announced.

Finally, our daughter's name – Melissa Rae Damsky. Oh, what a thrill hearing it! And oh what a joy it was to see her walk up those short steps and receive that hard-earned diploma as a part of Clarkson University's 112th graduation exercises.

And those incredible last words the president said before dismissing everyone, "And now, to all graduates, good luck and Godspeed."

Godspeed ... that got me.

And afterward ... trying to find her in that sea of people outside, as pictures were being taken, excitement and pride was everywhere, a parental dream come true.

Finally ... there she is!

The hug, the kiss, the affirmation of love, the posing for pictures we'll look at for years to come ... what a day.

Oh, what a glorious day!

**A proud papa with daughter Melissa at her
Clarkson University graduation, 2004**

Yain't Gonna Believe It

September 7, 2005

Over the years, I've preached at a number of local churches around here. One of them, the Hawkinsville Methodist Church, is a true small country church. You get to know the people there.

One of them, Melanie Yager, always had a great voice and I knew when I sang by myself there – when at those times the congregation sang along with me – I could depend on her strong voice to back me up.

She currently lives in Chicago and attends Moody Bible Institute.

She recently preached at our Methodist church here in Boonville. Just before she did, I spoke briefly with her. She told me she wasn't a preacher, and I completely understood, telling her that I wasn't either, but that, "You respond when you're asked."

I was anxious to hear her preach and she didn't disappoint. After the service, I approached her and told her how her sermon was absolutely terrific.

And she was.

In part of her sermon, she told of a phone conversation she had the previous evening with one of her girlfriends in Chicago. That girlfriend had a younger sister. That younger sister and her girlfriend went to a shopping center, but before going, the father of one of them warned them not to come home late from the shopping center because it wasn't in such a good neighborhood.

As Melanie commented at that part of her sermon, "When you're young like that, you don't pay that much attention to things like that."

The girls were two of the last to leave the shopping center. Their car seemed to be one of the only ones in the lot, parked a goodly distance from where they had exited the shopping center.

They decided to run to the car and while doing so, couldn't help but suddenly notice, from seemingly out of nowhere, several threatening-looking males running after them.

The scared girls made it to the car, got in and frantically locked the doors. They then tried to start the car, which wouldn't start. By this time, "the toughs" were at their car trying to get in, but try as the girls did, the car wouldn't start.

So they prayed.

They then tried starting the car – and, it started.

It was a terrifying experience, but they escaped.

When they got home, the father looked under the car hood and was stunned to see that the car had no battery!

When Melanie got to that part of her sermon, you could hear murmuring in the congregation. I was one of them.

I'll tell you what I think and you can make your own conclusion. And I'm not alone. I think it was nothing less than a modern-day miracle.

Oh … I called Jason Crill the next day. He owns a gas and service station here in Boonville. Over the years, he's proven to possess great automotive talent. But, even more so, he is a man of inspiring integrity.

I asked him if a car could start, much less run, without a battery.

He said, "Absolutely not."

So you tell me.

Bye Son

October 19, 2005

There ought to be a course taught to all of us, before we marry, that prepares us for how we will feel when the following happens with our children:

1. Their first day of kindergarten.
2. When they graduate from high school.
3. When they are dropped off at college.
4. When your son walks through airport security and disappears to board his plane that takes him to his Air National Guard Basic Training in Texas.

So that, when any of those things happen, especially number four, we're prepared ... unlike my wife and me recently.

We knew that parting would not – by any stretch – be considered a "bed of roses" ... more like "severe thorns".

And it isn't that my wife and I both didn't know that his leaving for Texas was for his own good. And, that everything we had prepared him for was for that farewell scene. And, that the next time we see him – in some six weeks when we fly to San Antonio for his graduation – he'll be a changed guy for the better.

Still ...

I looked up on the internet Norman Rockwell's illustration titled, "Breaking Home Ties." It shows how the father and his college-bound son are waiting for the train to arrive at their rural train station. The father has a look on his face, similar to the one my wife and I had on ours at the Syracuse Airport, before our son went through security. A look of – constrained helplessness.

Rockwell's portrayal of the son in that memorable illustration has an anticipated look of, "When's the train finally going to arrive so I can charge into the next exciting phase of my life?" That was the look my son Deane had at the Syracuse Airport.

You raise your children the best you know how, and it frequently doesn't all come out the way you'd like it to. And the dreams you have for them often end up being just that. It's easy to ignore that they have their own dreams. The time arrives and it doesn't take long when what you want – and what they want – is, well ... different.

And that alone is a message in humility, not that you care to admit you need it.

And you remember how you bucked your parents because you wanted to try life your way and express your true self in the way you wanted to ... needed to. And it's not that you didn't love them by not doing it their way, it was just that uncontrollable urge to be your own person ... the way they taught you to be as they raised you.

And then, there you are, walking away from airport security, dabbing your eyes, arm around your wife, not saying anything.

And knowing that, what you tried teaching him since he was born – to be independent and to, in fact, forge his own way with an emphasis on the noble way – worked.

Hallelujah! Right?

Still ...

Yes, Sir!

November 30, 2005

It's called River Walk, referred to by many as the "Venice of America".

It's right smack in the middle of downtown San Antonio, Texas. It's man-made. It's a winding miniature river about 35 feet wide, with shops, sidewalk cafes and restaurants on both sides. It has tour boats that continually depart for quiet 35-minute rides with tour guides pointing out the local history.

My wife, our son Deane and I were at River Walk on a recent late Friday afternoon. My wife was off visiting one of their many shops along the canal, leaving Deane and me to wander a bit by ourselves.

Frequently, total strangers seeing Deane in his Air Force uniform would approach and congratulate him. Being a military town, they knew he and his fellow brothers and sisters had just graduated from six weeks of basic training at nearby Lackland Air Force Base.

A casually dressed man, walking by, stopped and asked Deane if he had just graduated. When Deane told him he had, the man went on to explain his recent Air Force retirement as a Major General, returning from "Desert" that included Afghanistan and Iraq.

He asked Deane his home base, showing recognition when Deane told him, "Hancock Air Force Base in Syracuse, New York."

He inquired as to Deane's specialty, recognizing his "Aircraft Armament" response, and complimented him on his choice.

(Aircraft Armament is the loading of bombs to F-16 planes).

The man congratulated Deane, shook his hand and mine as well, and told him the Air Force needed good men like him. While walking away, he turned around saying, "Welcome aboard; we're glad to have you."

Deane looked at me and with wonder said, "Do you know how high up he is?"

I shrugged my shoulders and he continued, "He's a Two Star General!"

When observing Deane in his conversation with the general, I noticed an independent and confident quality I hadn't previously seen him have to that degree.

Deane told us stories concerning his fellow trainees, not all ending well. The military has its way of weeding out those who don't cut their "mustard". It's quite simple as you know. It's their way - or else.

The last night we were at his base, when walking to our car in the parking lot outside one of their stores, several female trainees ran up to one of their fellow trainee friends, passionately urging her to get back to her company immediately because she neglected to sign out and was listed as AWOL (Absent Without Official Leave). I asked Deane what they would do to her. He seemed to think they'd boot her out.

That girl – if that happened – will have the rest of her life to ponder her behavior.

For the three days my wife and I spent with Deane and observed him going through his military paces, one of the highlights was the stirring graduation exercises that ended with the announcer welcoming all the graduating trainees, "To the greatest Air Force the world has ever known."

It was another observational lesson in parental life that brought humbled tears to our eyes.

And in that blue uniform, allow me to say as a proud parent, he looked so grown up and oh, so handsome.

So another phase in our witnessing of our son's maturity flew by. Another forced "letting go" on our part – all for the better. Not entirely easy on our part, I might add.

You try to appreciate every moment of it.

**My son Deane's Basic Training graduation
at Lackland AFB in Texas, 11/18/05**

Eeny Meeny Miny Moe

December 14, 2005

It wasn't too long ago that my wife announced that we needed a new couch. I love my current couch and my wife, not in that order. Admittedly, I confess I put my couch time in. But I'm also not foolhardy to the elusive art of marriage, for I didn't even remotely question her new couch declaration.

Now there are those husbands out there who dictate every decision to their wives, at least I think I heard of one – well, maybe not.

So what's such a big deal about picking a new couch? You go to a store that sells them and buy one.

One, two, three … right?

Ahhhh … more like two, fourteen, six …

We went to the first store, a nice one. But try as we might, we came up empty.

So we went to three more furniture stores. Now, as you probably know, when you visit them, you can borrow pieces of material from each store. That way, of course, you try to envision how the new couch would look in your home from those small pieces.

Can you tell from those undersized examples? That's the gamble. And I don't even play cards. Oh, one thing — you have to be careful not to confuse bringing back the wrong pieces of couch material to the wrong stores. I'd care not to comment any further on that.

The first key to choosing a couch is the color. For the time you put into that alone, you could easily come to the conclusion that whatever color you may think you're looking for, doesn't exist.

But in your head or some other part of your body, you know there's got to be that perfect couch out there. It's just that the color you elusively seek is only known by a select few who currently reside in a distant tiny village in Zappa Koo-Koo. That's in Knee-Gee. Or is it Pablumsville?

So if a couch passes the possible color test, it's then the "sitting-down-on-it-for-comfort stage". If you magically pass that, there is a heightened sense of excitement as you then proceed into phase three … you lie down on it. But to do that, you have to take your shoes off and on repeatedly. And you soon come to the conclusion – you should really be wearing bedroom slippers because they're easier to take on and off.

The "lying-down-on-the-couch stage", or knowing the width and length is important if one wants to … snooze on it, for proper width and length to a frequent couch snoozer, is … vital.

Back to choosing the color of the couch.

It's easier finding a cure for dandruff.

And once you finally do choose the couch, right after that, you then really need to go away by yourself for a minimum of four years, to somewhere where all you do all day long is look out the window and sigh.

But I'm ecstatic to declare we finally found the perfect couch.

"They" should have furniture psychiatrists in the far corner of each couch store. I can see it now, "What's that doc, why am I wearing bedroom slippers?"

Dead What? Where?

January 18, 2006

As I was watching TV on a recent weekend morning, my wife walked in and announced, "We have a mouse in the cellar. I think it's dead. You'll have to get rid of it."

Coming from a family of non-hunters and in spite of Mickey Mouse and all the pleasure he's given humanity for so many years, the task did not thrill me.

I wanted to continue watching TV, but it wasn't an option.

Following the directions my wife gave me, I descended the cellar stairs with great trepidation. We have one of those homes where the cellar has a v-shaped ridge on the floor next to the outside walls. When there is water accumulation, it simply goes in that ridge and disappears out a centralized drain. It's an ancient system, but quite effective.

And there, beside our washing machine, in the ridge, lay permanent "Sleepy-Head."

And, hunter that I am not, I was there to extricate it.

It reminded me of when I was in college, and it was time to study. I'd look out the window, open up the refrigerator for perhaps the 77th time, scratch myself – anything to not have to study.

This was pretty much how it was in my preparation for "The Big Mouse Removal."

As I was checking my email, my wife – again – asked me if I had "done it."

I told her I needed time to prepare.

Let's put it this way … that wasn't the right answer.

Nor was my suggested plan of dispatch that included flushing

255 ❧

the little critter down the you-know-what.

So, with my winter coat on, armed with boots, plastic gloves, a large zip-lock bag and, as a backup, one of those plastic bags you get at grocery stores instead of "paper," I descended to where old "Mousey" lay.

My wife offered a coat hanger as a removal tool.

Her suggestion momentarily baffled me.

As I stood there planning my next move, I happened to notice on the floor, next to the washing machine, a pointed garden trowel my wife uses in non-winter times.

Utilizing the coat hanger to prod old "Mousy" into the garden trowel and carefully ascending the cellar stairs, I walked out through the not-so-deep snow with delicate care to the far backyard. When there, I gave the trowel, housing "Mickey Moto", a flicking swing and watched it sail to the furthest part of our back yard where in the summer, because of its thick foliage, no one goes.

Walking back into the house after the job was complete, I couldn't help but think of my brother-in-law who, in this past recent hunting season, skillfully bagged a 300-pound bear. But I had no less pride in my heart than he with his trophy, with my successful dispatch of "Little Louie", or perhaps "Lil Louise."

Upon re-entering the house, I shouted for my wife to hear, "The conquering hero has returned!" waiting for a thunderous response.

She was in the cellar out of listening range, so my victorious declaration went for naught.

But, in my heart, I knew my head-of-the-house responsibility lay intact, my paternal duties solid as a rock.

I may reassess my previous hunting apathy, for I think I'm now ready. Yes – I can see it now … wild boar - watch out!

Ahhhh -

Maybe not.

Old "Mousey's" Revenge

February 1, 2006

Let's see ... when you order a lobster at a restaurant, they put it in a pot and boil it. Sort of surprising to the unsuspecting lobster I suppose, but it hasn't altered how much lobster people eat.

It's the same with steamed clams. They're prepared the same way.

In both instances, the lobster and clams are alive as most of you know, when you put them in the boiling water.

A case for a similar situation could be made for throwing a four-legged creature into a ... fire.

In Fort Sumner, New Mexico, 81-year-old Luciano Mares caught a mouse inside his house and of course, wanted to dispose of it. Unlike my recent experience of finding a lifeless one in our cellar, Luciano's mouse was quite alive when he caught his.

The Jan. 9 article in the Utica *Observer-Dispatch* newspaper didn't report how he caught it, but that it was alive when he found it. The *Syracuse Post-Standard*, in their Jan. 12 edition, pointed out that the mouse was caught in a glue trap.

Now, here's where you question Luciano's 81 years of experienced reason and logic, for he then dispatched the live mouse, glue trap and all, into a pile of burning leaves he had near his house.

Do you think the mouse was happy about that?

Apparently not, for as many of you know having read or heard how it all ended, the mouse, by this time, was on fire. This, in turn, melted the glue trap the mouse was attached to. What may tip you off, if you had read, heard or seen any of the reports, was that this part of the story was told by Luciano, "from a motel room."

Why a motel room and not from his house?

Because on-fire "Mousey" ran back from the leaf fire it was thrown into and disappeared inside a window in Luciano's house. According to the *Syracuse Post-Standard*, "90 seconds later, the house was on fire." The next thing that happened was that Luciano's house and everything in it was destroyed by that fire.

The story didn't elucidate what happened to the on-fire mouse after the house burned down. It's possible, I suppose, that when the firemen came to put out the fire, some of their water doused flaming "Mousey" … who lives somewhere as these words are read.

Perhaps not.

But then again, Luciano has time to reflect on his choice of mouse removal.

Of course, we must give sufficient time to "Mousey", who perhaps in infinite wisdom, is either smiling alive scorched, or not.

If the fire prematurely ended its life, its headstone could read, "Here lies a vindicated mouse."

Oh, as far as eating lobster and clams are concerned, I'll have to think long and hard about ever doing that again.

Well, maybe not that long.

Mission Accomplished

April 26, 2006

On a Sunday some months ago, at church here in Boonville, Jeff Scherz told me that, as a Tech 5th Grade in the Third United States Army Division, he was there the day General George Patton led his fellow soldiers as they entered and liberated one of World War II's largest concentration camps in Germany – Buchenwald.

And that even though he wasn't supposed to – knowing his camera would be taken from him if he did – Jeff, nevertheless, took pictures of what he saw. They did take his camera, but not before he took the film out and, shortly thereafter, had it developed in nearby Weimar.

I could hardly believe what he was telling me. He asked me if I knew where those pictures could be sent.

I told Jeff about my cousin, Elaine, who lived in Israel, who could possibly help. He was encouraged by that and made a point of urging me to see those pictures. Sensing what Jeff's pictures would show, it took me some time to get the courage to view them. In the meantime, I had emailed my cousin in Israel, who also instructed me to view the pictures and after that, she'd lead me to her friend who worked in Washington, DC.

Some months ago, I went to Jeff's house and viewed the pictures. They were as penetrating as I guessed them to be.

Thus began a series of emails between my cousin in Israel, her friend in Washington, and me. That friend, in turn, led me to her fellow co-worker, Rebecca Erbelding, the archivist of the United States Holocaust Memorial Museum in Washington, DC. I have been communicating with Rebecca for some months now.

It ended up that the museum requested that Jeff donate two pictures of his collection to the museum, borrowing a quote from one of Rebecca's emails, "Where they will be available for scholars, researchers and visitors in perpetuity." I looked up the word "perpetuity" just to be sure I knew its meaning. Our *Webster's Dictionary* reads, "Endless or indefinitely long duration or existence."

Each of the two pictures is of a building with a different banner hanging from each one. One picture shows the U.S. troops as they approached the entrance to Buchenwald with a building in the background. The banner on that building translated from German reads, "Day of Antifascism Fight." The other picture shows a building with a banner directing war correspondents to where they should go.

The museum had pictures of those buildings similar to Jeff's, but what distinguished Jeff's pictures from all the rest was that none had the banners on them his did.

During one of our email communications, Rebecca wrote, "As the news in Iran conveys, Holocaust denial is still a big issue. Having the original photographs whenever possible is a way to combat potential charges of photo editing."

So Jeff's pictures are added proof that what happened in Buchenwald actually happened. And the world can view those pictures, along with others, which undeniably prove the horror of the Buchenwald concentration camp.

In my research I learned that General Eisenhower said, concerning the troops who liberated Buchenwald, "If America's soldiers didn't know before what they were fighting for, at least now they knew what they were fighting against. These soldiers felt very proud that they had arrived in time to stop this unbelievable cruelty before the rest of the prisoners in the camp could be fed into the Nazi killing machine. Even better, they had stopped the ugly bigotry and racism of the Germans before American citizens could be subjected to a similar fate."

Eisenhower at his finest.

How many of us can point to something in life we've contributed to ... that carries on in perpetuity ... something for all the world to see and examine, something of grave significant historical importance? How often has it been said of the Holocaust, for all to remember it – so that it never happens again?

Jeff Scherz has contributed to that.

Oh, during his Army career, Jeff also participated in the "Battle of the Bulge" and was also in the first wave at the "Landing in Normandy."

And he's absolutely one of the nicest guys you'd ever want to meet.

Jeff Scherz is a hero. Thank you a million times, Jeff, and thank you to all the soldiers who fought and continue to this day to fight against tyranny and injustice.

Play It Again, Meowsa

May 10, 2006

For well over the past seven months, I've been driving to Syracuse on selected Saturdays to Andy Rudy's house, where I have been recording the tracks and my singing for a gospel CD of original songs. I currently have the basics recorded for nine songs, with a few more to go. After that, the next phase enters with the auditioning and recording of background singers.

The room that we record in has a small couch where I put my electronic piano. On one side of this room is Andy's upright piano. Against the far wall is his electronic piano and recording equipment. When he is recording individual parts to one of the songs – bass, drums, etc. – he sits on one end of the upright piano bench and, at times, I'll sit on the other end at the same time playing along with him on his upright piano. The reason I mention these details is to lay the groundwork for Andy's cat, Meowsa.

You never know what she's going to do.

One Saturday, she didn't show herself to me. She was in the house somewhere, but for cat reasons we'll never know, passed on seeing me.

But most of the time, she'll appear.

In one instance, when I was ready to return home, I took the electronic piano from the couch, carrying it to the next room only to see Meowsa nestled comfortably in its open traveling case. The cat's attitude was, "Disturb me not!"

Another time, my electronic piano was on the couch and Andy and I were discussing some detail of what we were working on. Suddenly, we heard a musical sound we both didn't recognize.

Not only was it musically unusual but, since we weren't playing anything, the obvious question was, where was the strange musical noise coming from?

Looking around, it didn't take us long to figure out the mystery. There was Meowsa walking on my turned on electronic piano keyboard, playing whatever notes she was stepping on. You would think when she heard the music, which she was in essence making, she'd be frightened and jump off. But she kept walking … groovin.

Maybe she could end up being the world's first feline piano virtuoso. But from what we heard that day, she needs some work.

Now the highlight is when Andy and I are "red hot" into recording whatever it is at the moment we're working on. You could say the creative juices are running on high, and it is usually at those times I'm singing into the microphone, standing up facing Andy's back. At those intense moments, Meowsa appears, sitting on Andy's piano bench just next to where I'm standing.

What makes it so unusual is her attitude when that happens, for at those heightened moments, she sits there, her head stretching up, looking at me in a most committed and involved way. It's as if she's totally enfolded in the creative moment as much as Andy and I are. Who knows … maybe more. You've got to see it. It's as if she's silently saying, "How absolutely fascinating! More! More! You're doing great!" And when she does it, and I happen to look down and see her looking at me with her involved encouragement, I crack up.

Meowsa.

When it's complete, I should give her a credit on the CD.

What Seats!

October 11, 2006

"You're going to love the seats, as they're right on the 50-yard line," my oldest brother said.

He has season's tickets to the Syracuse University football games. He calls me on those rare occasions when he can't attend. If we're able to go, my wife and I jump at the chance. He called a couple of weeks ago, when Syracuse played Wyoming at the Syracuse Dome, offering us his tickets, and we went.

My wife and I split up before the game to do some shopping near where the game would be played. I happened to arrive at the Dome first. A man, one seat over in front of me who looked to be in his late 60s, turned around and – with gusto – told me his son would be arriving shortly and would be sitting in back of me. He described him as being quite boisterous, and intimated his sympathy for me because of that.

Shortly, thereafter, his son arrived, whereupon the father jokingly yelled to him how he should act a bit more reserved because I was sitting in front of him.

My wife arrived and as other fans around us filled in as well, we later guessed many were either relatives of the father in front of me, or very dear friends who come to all the football games and who sounded quite knowledgeable about the game. At various times during the contest, they exchanged seats with each other.

One thing that stood out among their various extroverted personalities was their appreciation and loyalty for the "hops".

For the first two quarters beer was allowed to be sold, various members of the group descended, only to shortly return with four plastic cups of the Dome's finest brew. One time, as one shuffled by us returning from a "hops" run, I whispered to my wife, "Those four beers cost $18."

The son in back of me, since it was an unusually exciting game, would yell whatever he felt like as the game progressed. He would frequently elicit a howling "Yaahhhh!" that definitely got one's attention, particularly ours.

The game was very close and each team scored effortlessly. The first time Syracuse was called on to attempt what turned out to be a successful 42-yard field goal, the response from the son in back of us was a thunderous, "We've got a kicker!"

The second time Syracuse kicked a successful long field goal, the father in front of us passionately whooped, "We've got a kicker!"

And the trips to the "hops" vendor kept up at a pace that race car drivers at the Indianapolis 500 could only dream of ... none purchasing less than four at a time.

Financially, I figured they were all in the top tax bracket ... or, deeply overextended.

I've thus far neglected to tell you about the high-fives that followed each time Syracuse scored. Since the game ended in a thrilling, double-overtime 40 to 34 win for Syracuse, the high-fiving was at a feverous pitch. When they did it, the father would get up, stretch past me and high-five his son, who in turned reached over me and high-fived the relative/friend/who-knows-what, next to him.

The second to the last touchdown, they all broke down and took my wife and me into their little exclusive high-fiving circle.

We had arrived.

The seats? They were the best I've ever had to see a football game.

I hope my brother comes through with some future tickets for it'll be good to see – oh – the old gang.

By the way, they were right. We've got a kicker!

Did You See How Close He Came?

January 10, 2007

The night before the last day of 2006, my family attended the Syracuse/St. Bonaventure basketball game at the Carrier Dome. Arriving there with some time to spare before the game, I suggested we all go down to courtside and watch the SU players do their warm-up shooting where you could see them up close. We all went down and while standing there, watching SU shoot not 20 yards away, a college-aged gentleman with a clipboard approached my son Deane, explaining to him that if he accepted, he would be the lone person – at halftime – to stand at center court and attempt two shots at the basket. If he made one, he'd receive a $500 gift certificate to the campus book store. He then asked Deane if he was interested in trying it.

Deane politely declined.

When he did, I said to him, "I think you'd enjoy it ... it would be fun and, besides, what do you have to lose?"

My daughter Melissa added, "Yeah, Deane, it would be fun - you should do it."

I put in a last ditch, "You've got nothing to lose."

We all anxiously awaited his decision, and after some hesitation, he responded, "OK, I'll try it."

The gentleman took Deane's information and carefully explained where they'd meet four minutes before halftime.

The first half of the game was very close and went by quickly. My wife tugged my arm pointing to Deane and his sister descending the steps to where he was to meet the gentleman with the clipboard, signaling it was four minutes before the end of the half.

I asked my wife why Melissa was going with him and was told she was going to take pictures of what happened on Deane's cellphone.

The half ended and several events then took place.

A spectator rolled two giant dice at mid-court. The dice he threw matched and he won.

Next, a man – while lying on a recliner positioned just below the basket, had two chances to shoot a basketball through the hoop lying on the recliner. On the second try, he was successful and won the recliner.

A couple of pre-teen girls competed against each other on opposite sides of the court, dribbling back and forth, putting on oversized shorts while doing so. One did it more expediently than the other, sinking the basket first - the winner.

The announcer next stated for all to turn their attention to center court, "Where two half-court shots would be taken by Deane Damsky of Boonville … who, if successful, would win a $500 gift certificate from the campus book store."

Accompanied by the gentleman with the clipboard, Deane walked from the mid-court sideline to the center of the court, as two huge overhead screens showed him doing so. They showed a close-up of Deane, and he looked like any young leading man of any movie.

At that moment, there wasn't a prouder pappy.

He then took his first of two shots, coming up short.

His second attempt brushed the bottom of the net as the crowd responded with a collective gasp.

The announcer continued, "Let's give Deane Damsky, all the way from Boonville, a big Carrier Dome hand," as the two screens showed him up close walking off the court, as 20,000 plus enthusiastically responded.

Thrilling?
Oh my!
And to top it off, Syracuse won the game.
'Twas an unforgettable night.

Playing the Hand You're Dealt

August 8, 2007

I met an encouraging, inspiring person recently. Actually, we've been acquaintances for 10 years, but we only recently broke through getting to know each other better.

He is a graphic artist.

Tom Yacovella is his name.

Since I'm in the advertising business, one of my jobs is to find the best person to create logos for our clients.

Tom does great logos.

At nine years of age, his mother passed away. His father couldn't support him and his three younger siblings, and because his father was a Mason, all four were brought up at the Masonic Home.

When Tom was of college age, he did so well at Utica's Proctor High School, he earned a full scholarship to Syracuse University, majoring in advertising design.

There, he blazed an educational swath of accomplishments graduating magna cum laude.

His main professor of advertising insisted Tom seek work in New York City, the mecca for advertising, emphasizing he'd be in the middle of his aspiring profession.

So Tom went to New York, stayed at the YMCA with $55.00 in his pocket, money raised at a going away party his uncle organized.

One of Tom's first friends in New York urged him to contact David Rockefeller, the president of all eighty Chase Manhattan Banks.

You really don't just drop in and see David Rockefeller.

But Tom is Tom, and making it to David's secretary – a feat in itself – he then explained to her how he and his brother and two sisters were brought up at Utica's Masonic Home. He also mentioned that he was an aspiring graphic artist and wanted to show David his college work. When the secretary imparted that information to David, also a Mason, he brought Tom into his office, which Tom described as "carpeting so plush, it was like walking on a cloud."

After showing David Rockefeller samples of his college work, David offered to call one of the advertising agencies Chase Manhattan used.

It didn't take Tom long to spend the $55. Running out of money, he was actually packing his bags when the call for the interview came through from the advertising agency David Rockefeller had contacted.

You can't make up stuff like this.

At that interview, the secretary told him that they had no intention of hiring him and that he was only being seen as a favor to David Rockefeller. When interviewed, Tom was told they had sixteen graphic artists and weren't looking for more. But, after seeing his work, Tom said they made room for him, hiring him as their seventeenth graphic artist.

They made room for him.

The sixteen graphic artists had seniority and because of that, Tom wasn't given the bigger jobs, only the entry-level ones, even though his work was immediately published in the best of magazines.

After three months working there, Tom went to the head of the firm.

As you can see, Tom's something else.

Tom showed him the work he'd been doing for the firm, which

Tom felt wasn't nearly up to what he could really do. Tom then asked the head of the firm that when bigger projects came up, if he could be given the opportunity to show what he could do, and that he'd do that work in his spare time at home. He was given that chance, and sure enough, Tom became most successful.

Tom eventually made it back to his Mohawk Valley roots and has continued to do extraordinary work.

Wait until you see the logo he just completed for Old Forge, New York. It's absolutely terrific. You'll be seeing a lot of it as the years roll by.

Tom's story sheds light on humanity's potential. Tom had a choice in his less than desirable life growing up. He could have moaned and complained about what he didn't have, but instead put that same energy into the potential he was handed.

Let Tom serve as an inspiration for us all.

Wondering – Uh Oh ...

January 16, 2008

I wonder.

A lot.

For instance, since this is the year the country votes for a new president, will we change history by voting in a woman?

Do I eat too much chocolate?

Can the Syracuse Orangemen – with such a young basketball team – mature enough by the end of the season to successfully grapple with the heavyweights of the Big East and beyond?

Can a bathroom scale possibly possess obnoxious qualities?

How high will gas prices really go?

There's proof that laughing helps keep away sickness.

Ha, ha, ha, ha ...

If a car battery could talk, just before expiring, would it say, "Goodbye, cruel world."

Can you laugh yourself silly?

Is there a level of winter beauty yet to be seen?

What's it like to lie on a warm beach right about now?

What it's like to scale Mount Everest?

Could a pill take the place of food?

What's the next great movie to come out, and will I go see it when it does?

When's the last time I went to a movie?

What makes a lightning bug ... a lightning bug?

Will there be a substitute for gas that will straighten out those rich oil sheiks?

What it's like to have oil sheik money?

Will it be Obama as our next president?

There's a line in an old song that says, "I wonder, wonder, wonder, wonder, who wrote the book of love?" Who could that have been?

Yep, I wonder.

If I wonder too much, do I miss life?

Ha, ha, ha, ha …

Do people run out of gas anymore?

Can you think too much, and if so, does the brain do something you'd prefer it wouldn't?

Isn't the January thaw we recently had sweeter than sugar?

What if they could tame a tornado and turn its fury into energy?

Just think how this earth we live in is spinning in space. And nothing shakes or spills. I wonder if the scientists have that right.

Will they ever figure out how the pyramids were built? I talked to someone who recently visited them. He said it was the most amazing thing he's ever seen. Were these guys fishing on the Nile and one of them said, "Let's build a few pyramids?" There must have been one guy who said, "How?"

Why can't they build a car that's powered by water?

What if every day was like Saturday?

What if every day was like Sunday?

We know about Monday.

Is it possible one fish – in its own language – would say to another, "I've had it with swimming!"

Was the guy's last name – who invented them – Dungarees? "You have a hole in your dungarees, Mr. Dungarees."

Can dreams be truly sweet?

I keep trying to remember, when I dream, if it's in color. I hope so. I asked someone recently if she dreamt in color. Even though I knew she heard me, she said, "What?" Walking away, I heard her say, "I never heard of such a thing."

I wonder if I should end here.

Ha, ha, ha, ha …

There He Is! There He Is!

August 13, 2008

A couple of months ago, we saw my son Deane off to Iraq at Hancock Air Force Base in Syracuse. He had volunteered with others from his base for eight weeks of active duty in Balad, Iraq, 35 miles from Baghdad.

So these past number of weeks – our family, relatives and friends – have been mindful of him being in a war zone.

That'll take you off stride.

But the reports from him via instant messaging and occasional phone calls soothed our anxieties, and sure enough there we were last week, back at Hancock Air Force Base in Syracuse, to receive him from completing his active duty – back on safe soil.

There were between 200 and 300 troops on the jumbo plane that arrived in the early evening. When the plane landed, the clapping and ecstatic shouting began. As the plane taxied and stood motionless before the troops exited, there was great excitement and emotion in the air. As they departed the plane, the shouts and clapping picked up in intensity.

I guessed an estimated 700 relatives and friends were present to receive the troops, all waiting anxiously for their military loved ones to walk through an entranceway in that large Air Force hangar. As that happened, everyone clapped and shouted and frequently children, sweethearts, and wives broke away from the roped off area, emotionally running to them and embracing them.

It was very powerful – very powerful. No one had to be reminded of appreciating their loved one's safe return from a faraway war zone such as the hot spot that is Iraq.

What seemed like an eternity came to fruition about an hour and a half after the plane landed, when Deane finally walked into the hangar. As each soldier appeared, everybody clapped, particularly the family and friends of each soldier. When Deane finally came through, we clapped and shouted our joy with the others. And, seeing him smile to that reception, well – it was worth the absolute world knowing he was safely back home.

On our way home on the thruway, he said he couldn't wait to take a long hot shower.

It's the little things in life.

His daily job at his Iraq air base was maintaining the apparatus that holds the bombs to the planes, working 12-hour shifts, six days a week for the couple of months he was there.

He handed out some gifts on the way home, one to his mother of a small wooden camel of respectful detail. That camel came a long way.

Deane said he was going to sleep for several days.

It was a most emotional experience welcoming him back home. It brought attention to those who give of themselves for the security we all take for granted.

We're so grateful Deane's out of harm's way and for the selfless giving he and all soldiers everywhere offer for the preciousness we all know as liberty and freedom.

And, seeing him come through the entranceway of that giant hangar, I have a new and clearer understanding of what pride means.

For him, and for all those from his air base and of course for all those not only in Iraq, Afghanistan and all war zones, who on a daily basis, offer their lives in essence for all of us, a hearty - **HIP HIP HOORAY** for all who serve for our freedom! May God truly bless them all!

Deane in sandy Iraq. An anxious time, 2008

Hope

August 27, 2008

I've just completed the most challenging project of my life.

Over three years ago, I decided to save as much money as I could and record a CD of the best of over 150 gospel songs I had written over the past dozen plus years.

My reasoning was that the gospel/inspirational music industry would possibly take my songs more seriously if I had a complete body of work, rather than how they were taking me with the two songs I had recorded up to that time, and they weren't taking those very seriously.

So I set about accomplishing what I had no idea would take so much time to do with so much money to do it. Money I didn't have at the time. I had enough to slowly put it together, but not nearly enough for what I later found out I needed.

But in the last several years, financially, life went my way and suddenly the money appeared. Gospel songs are songs of faith, so I wrote off the money coming my way as faith fulfilled, with a hearty Hallelujah, I might add!

Along that long and demanding route, one of the biggest challenges I faced, to make the sound of the songs complete, was to find background singers. I tracked down three singers, recording them on several songs. The sound was solid, but those singers had lives that didn't include further recording. Not meant to be.

I found a Syracuse musical choir director who selected six singers from his church choir and through his musical tutelage, recorded them on most of the 16 songs in the form of a CD entitled, *We Declare*. There is one song on the CD, "Sinful Temptation", produced and recorded five years ago in Nashville, Tennessee, with Nashville background singers.

A website for the CD is up and running. Anyone interested, by going to BarryDamsky.com, can hear 'tastes' of each song and can view all the lyrics and comments on each song. The viewer, if interested, can acquire the CD itself and even download as many of the songs as he or she wishes.

One of the perks the company offered that duplicated the CD is what they call a "sampler," a CD sent to about 500 gospel/inspirational musical industry insiders in the form of radio stations, record companies, etc. That sampler also has a song from 21 artists just like me. So it's possible that the song I picked, "We Declare," the title song, will stir some of those industry insiders and "a break" will emerge from it.

I'm as energized over the possible ramifications of the CD as I've ever been about anything I've attempted in my life.

I'd like to get the songs to established singers who might consider recording any of the songs, getting my music out to the public that way.

And if no singer is interested in doing that, I'll just go sing the songs where doors open.

Anyway, that's the dream. And not to get too heavy here, but whatever happens, good, bad or otherwise, all glory, praise and honor go to God through his son Jesus, not only with this CD, but with everything.

An Unscheduled Dancing Guest

August 5, 2009

All week, I checked the weather for the upcoming Syracuse performance with the results the same – scattered thunderstorms. The morning of that performance, my wife informed me that hail was possible. Hail in July.

When it was my time to go up on stage, I walked up the side steps and stood off to one side, waiting to be introduced.

As the pastor, who organized the gospel festival at the Inner Harbor in Syracuse, was thanking Keith Copes for leading me to that festival, Keith was standing near me in the back of the stage. Suddenly, the preacher stopped introducing me and spoke directly to a 30ish looking African-American man standing below on the ground in front of the stage.

I heard the pastor hesitate and then say, "You want to give testimony?" with the man responding he would. The pastor then directed the man to come up on stage.

The man slowly and laboriously limped around the side and almost couldn't make it up the stairs. He had one foot and arm fully bandaged. He finally made it to the microphone and then told the story of his past week and how he gave a man $40 to buy a car. The man he gave the money to suddenly left, driving off with his $40 and the car.

He explained how he called the man who took his money and car and told him he was going to meet him and beat him up. He went on to tell how he then met him with heated words being exchanged. The man with the car and money then took out and pointed a gun at him, pulling the trigger, but it jammed.

He then said how he jumped on him, and during the struggle, the gun went off, not hitting anyone. The police came, both were taken to jail and the guy with the gun was jailed. The man telling the story was released.

He went on to further tell how days later, when he was driving, a car suddenly cut in front of him so close that he had to swerve to avoid hitting that car. In doing so, he had the choice of either hitting someone on a bicycle or hitting a tree. He chose the tree. The result was broken bones, thus the reason for the heavily bandaged foot and arm.

The pastor directed that bandaged man to Keith Copes and then finished introducing me.

As I was singing, I noticed one of the singers who had sung prior to me, dancing on the ground beneath me near the front of the stage, with what I guessed to be her 6 or 7-year-old daughter leading the dancing.

I could also see a middle-aged woman below me who moved rhythmically to the music.

Performing my fourth and final song – midway through – something caught my attention out of the corner of my eye. Turning, I saw a girl who looked to be 9 or 10, unabashedly dancing on stage for all to see – just feet from me – who continued doing so until the song ended.

Afterward, the pastor told me that he wanted to produce the second Syracuse Gospel Fest next year at Armory Square in downtown Syracuse and that he wanted me to be a part of it.

Oh, as I was walking to my car, the skies opened up and it rained, like it outrageously poured, complete with thunder and lightning. Man, did it come down.

No hail though.

Let's Not Get Too Crazy

July 7, 2010

Perhaps you might have heard about the 60 pianos located all over New York City for a recent piano exhibit, where anybody off the street could sit down and play.

On the second day of that exhibit, while watching the television news, it showed New Yorkers playing on some of those pianos, some singing their hearts out.

After that newscast, I sat down at my piano and played and sang whatever came into my heart, which is what I usually do. While I was doing that, I thought of the New York piano exhibit, figuring how much it would cost to go there and the time it would take.

I further thought how I should go to New York fantasizing how I would be discovered for the singer/songwriter/piano player I – sometimes more than others – think I am.

As I sat at my piano, the next thing I knew I was singing the '60s song recorded by Ben E. King with The Drifters, "Save the Last Dance for Me." It's about a guy who takes his sweetheart to a dance and tolerates her dancing with others, only to remind her that he has the last dance with her, and it's in his arms she's going to be, not any one of the guys he's letting her dance with.

A possible insight into the song was that one of the two writers, Doc Pomus, had polio. He used crutches to get around and couldn't dance. His wife was a Broadway actress and dancer.

It had been some time since I sang that song and recalled only a portion of the lyrics, so I went on the internet and tracked them down.

It was back in the '80s and I was living in Los Angeles. I was typing at UCLA to pay my bills. One day, I was in one of their cafeterias and found myself walking behind a teen-aged, male African-American. I could lightly hear him singing a song.

He sounded great, so I stopped him, telling him how I felt he had such a fine voice, further telling him I was an aspiring singer. He told me he was a member of a young rock band, with the result of that conversation ultimately leading me to drive to the inner city of Los Angeles where he and his group rehearsed. Their manager was there with the group, which consisted of a drummer, a bass player and a guitar player.

At a break during their rehearsal, I started teaching them my version of the song, "Save the Last Dance for Me." It didn't take long for the group to catch on and it started to sound pretty cool. At that moment, the manager stepped in, most frustrated I had interrupted the group's rehearsal.

I politely said my farewells but always remembered that there was life in my version of that song.

After having seen New Yorkers on television singing and playing pianos all over that city, as I sat at my piano singing and playing "Save the Last Dance for Me," I thought that if I were to go to New York before the exhibit ended July 5, and sing and play, I'd be discovered.

Did I go and did that happen?

No.

Some might ask, "Why didn't you go?"

My response to them would be that I'd just have to be discovered some other way.

Action!

August 4, 2010

A bit less than two years ago, I released *We Declare*, a CD of my gospel songs.

Since then, I wrote a video script I envisioned would go along with the music to one of the songs on that CD, "What Do You Want?"

A year ago, I was in the process of working up a new song in Syracuse for further recording purposes. Andy Rudy, whom I do that with and who helped me create my entire CD, asked me how the CD, *We Declare* was doing. I told him it wasn't doing well. He then suggested I do a music video of one of my songs from that CD, commenting "that would then kick the CD off."

When he said it, something in me resonated, and I enthusiastically told him I already had written a script for one.

Six months ago, I committed myself to making that script into a finished music video for release in DVD form.

And the doors started opening, not always the case with projects I have tried.

Most of the video was filmed here in Boonville with the remainder in Utica.

I showed that video to some people I trusted and each had varying opinions, all having one thing in common ... encouragement.

I recently finished editing the video. At the same time, I submitted it to a TV station in Atlanta that airs spiritual musical videos. I'll continue to do that with other TV stations which also do that, wherever they may be.

Whatever TV station accepts it for viewing would be a big

break for the video, hopefully spurring interest in the CD. It remains to be seen who will, if any, accept it. I've got hope.

You can see that video if you go on your computer and google, "You Tube, Barry Damsky, *What Do You Want?*

Of the 10 actors in the video, none would consider themselves professional or even aspiring actors. Nine of them were recommended by people whose opinions I respected; the tenth, my son Deane, you could say I recommended.

Everybody in the video is just terrific. When you see the video, I hope you'll agree.

Since I'm an independent artist, that is, do not have an established record company label I recorded my CD with, no major radio stations will play my music. But I had no choice if I wanted to make the CD. So I recorded it on my own, taking my chances that someone - somewhere - would "discover" it and off it would go. Well – that hasn't happened and it may never.

By producing the DVD of one of the songs from the CD, my hope and prayer is that a TV station that airs that type of music, will "discover" it by playing it, and the hoopla from that would spur interest in my CD, *We Declare* – sort of a roundabout way of getting the CD off the ground.

That's my latest dream.

Time will obviously tell how it all comes out, but I must admit, in any event, it's one of the more exciting times of my life.

Yes, Dear

October 13, 2010

My wife and I recently attended the nearby annual Remsen Barn Festival.

The plan was to take a shuttle bus from their enormous parking lot to their main street where all the action took place. When we parked, we overheard some people next to us mention you could walk down a steep hill and over a field, getting there that way. My wife liked that idea remarking, "You need the exercise." I told her I'd prefer to take the shuttle, knowing it was a useless effort.

So we walked down that steep and rather long hill across a field and then found ourselves at the beginning of the street, where countless booths on both sides of that street were located, literally selling everything from soup to nuts.

Just watching the people streaming in was interesting, and frequently, we saw dogs led by their masters. As the crowd got thicker, I felt sorry for those dogs having to maneuver through that tangled crowd. At one particularly thick crowd moment, my wife pointed to a middle-aged male, inches in front of me, wearing a backpack. In that backpack, peering at me silently, wearing a hat, bandana and sunglasses, was a tiny dog looking so cool. If dogs could talk, my guess was, that dog would have asked me if I wanted to play cards. Poker.

As it got to be late morning, hunger beckoned. Before purchasing a bison burger, I asked a young gentleman eating one if he liked it; he admitted he did. I then asked him what it tasted like. He responded, "It's a cross between a hamburger and sausage."

Since I like both, I thought that to be an irresistible sales pitch.

Did it taste like that? More like a hamburger; a good one, but nonetheless, a hamburger.

My food quest not satiated, we came upon a booth it didn't take long to figure out should be on every street corner wherever one lives – one that featured freshly baked chocolate chip cookies.

I wondered if heaven has chocolate chip cookies, figuring it must, otherwise it wouldn't be called heaven.

One of my life quests has been the unrelentless search for a better chocolate chip cookie. Those that day were superb. I can now die happy.

Not one to let go of a good idea, I thought about my return pass and finding the booth that sold those delectable cookies.I suspected the crowd would make that quest most challenging, well... you want to guess what happened?

If your response was I couldn't find that booth, you get 100.

Is my life incomplete not having enjoyed that cookie encore?

I'll give you a hint – yes.

Did we walk over that field and back up that long hill or take the shuttle?

I'll give you another hint. I wanted to take the shuttle bus.

A last hint and I'll let you go.

What's it like to want?

The Executioner

December 8, 2010

It was a recent early October Friday evening when I arrived home
… hungry. No big deal.

As I sat in the kitchen eating dinner, I thought I saw something …something flying.

As my dinner proceeded, it happened again … confirming it
was a fly.

Ever since I saw a film many years ago, while attending Army
Basic Training, that showed the incredible amount of germs flys
carry, they have been a passionate part of my life's extermination
routine.

At a later point during that dinner, it flew by once again, this
time irking me to a more serious approach to its hopeful demise,
thus prompting me to seek out the "killing machine" hung in our
cellar doorway. Yes, if used properly, the effective fly swatter.

As the evening progressed, it must have gone to sleep or found
someone else to bother, for I saw it no more.

I get up early – sometimes earlier than at other times. It's just
a pattern I follow. I never know what I'm going to write or when
I'm going to write it. You could say it's the strange life of a writer.
Either that or I need to be committed.

And so it went that next early morning, reading the Utica paper in front of my computer.

I noticed some exterior movement and looking up saw what
I guessed to be the unwanted flying houseguest. It landed on the
computer tower next to where I sat.

I rose, careful not to disturb it, slowly walking into the

adjoining kitchen where the fly swatter lay from the previous evening. I took a couple of practice swings with it, slamming it on top of the chair in the kitchen, sensing I was too far away to disturb the wretch in seventh sleeping heaven on the computer tower. Invigorated with the thrill of the quest, I returned with it to the back room – noticing on the way – that the clock on the wall read 4 a.m. As I walked by it, I thought to myself, "Death at 4 a.m."

I stealthily arrived back to the computer area and there it was – still on top of the computer tower.

Taking careful aim, with great passion, I struck. When I did, I noticed it rose from the tower, leading me to believe I had missed it; but a moment later, it was clear it had only risen from the force I hit it with. It dropped to the floor. Yup ... "deader than Abe Lincoln".

I felt triumphant, although there was no one around to share my combative glory.

Death at 4 a.m. could be the title of a book. Perhaps, *Death at 3:57 a.m.* although it doesn't seem to have the same flair.

I think I like, *The Fly Riseth*.

Casabubu on World Politics and More

January 12, 2011

And, out of nowhere, as I was about to get into my car at the supermarket, I heard his unmistakable voice saying, "Bah-ree, I can't believe it's you."

There's no mistaking that voice, much less attitude, for who should it be?

You guessed it! My old friend Casabubu ...

"Cas!" I exclaimed. "How you been, you old dog you!"

Flashing his pearly whites, dazzling in themselves, he responded, "If I was any better, I'd be an orangutan."

I wasn't sure how to take that, but knowing Casabubu as I have for so many years, I just let it go.

An orangutan.

"Bah-ree, that Chinese Nobel Peace Prize winner, Liu Xiaobo ... I noticed China didn't let him out of prison, putting his wife under house arrest so neither could accept his prize."

"I read about it", I sadly lamented.

He continued, "Twas most dramatic how at the Peace Prize ceremony in Norway, Liu's chair stood on that dais, empty, in front of that giant photograph of him."

I told him it was very disheartening.

He continued, "And how the head guy there put Liu's prize on that lonely Nobel awards chair. And how China's media went off the air at the precise moment those ceremonies started. And they think the world doesn't see them for what they are."

I told him we shouldn't forget Liu and the sacrifices he's made for freedom and liberty, particularly at the cost of his own.

"Bah-ree," he went on. "It goes to show the power of the pen and how it can be a two-edged sword. Now here sits Liu in a Chinese prison just because he wrote about how he saw China someday being free to self-expression and all the freedoms we take for granted in these incredible United States of ours. So he writes for freedom and gets thrown in jail; it just doesn't make sense."

I told Casabubu at that point, that we can't imagine in our wildest dreams, what it's like to live in a Communist state like China. And that we should all be dancing in the streets because we can speak, write and sing – the truth.

Changing subjects, I asked him, "How about Boonville being the second snowiest in America?" He responded he had also read how the Weather Channel recently published that Boonville has an average of 220.5 inches of snow a year.

"But don't forget, Cas," I reminded him. "We're not #1, just a humble #2."

Nothing escapes Casabubu as he affirmed, "You're right, only Valdez, Alaska, averages more with 297.7 inches a year."

I told him we're all famous, being a part of the second snowiest in the country, right here in little old Boonville.

"It's a challenge to live here," I told him, continuing, "One that makes you feel good you survived."

Cas then remarked that they should have T-shirts that say, "I survived another Boonville winter."

I told him that was a great idea.

So, if you see T-shirts suddenly appearing that says that, know Casabubu is making some extra spending money.

Casabubu … a possible business titan.

A Break - Possibly - Maybe?

March 23, 2011

On the way to work recently, I heard a song on my car radio whose singer sounded familiar. I hadn't heard that voice in many a year and thought how it sounded like a Christian singer Fernando Ortega.

One of the benefits of having satellite radio in the car is that the name of who is singing and the name of the song are shown on the small screen on the radio. The singer's name read Fernando Ortega.

What a voice that man has!

It was 10 years ago, the day my daughter graduated from high school. That afternoon, we had a party in the backyard, complete with a tent.

The following is a good portion of what I wrote about, at the end of that momentous day.

"As I was driving away from the high school grounds after the graduation ceremonies, as prearranged, I called Pastor Bill Mudge on my cellphone, and he told me he would be at my house in 15 minutes to accompany me to Syracuse.

And we went, taking an hour.

Upon entering the Syracuse Christian bookstore, I noticed a table was set up in the front of the store. On it was a cake with a likeness of Fernando on the top. Fernando then appeared, sitting down behind that table.

A short line quickly formed for those who wanted to talk to him, and I stood at the end of that line, waiting my turn to do the same.

Bill stood off to the side of the table with my camera. When my turn came, I shook Fernando's hand and told him I had just driven some distance from Boonville and that my daughter graduated from high school hours earlier. I further told him I wrote spiritual songs, one I had with me, entitled "Forevermore", on cassette for his performing and/or recording consideration. Getting my music to someone of his international stature could be my big break. He seemed appreciative when I handed my cassette to him, and I felt there was a good chance he would listen to it.

He asked if I was going to attend his concert that night. I told him that I had to get back home to my daughter's graduation party. He was most sympathetic thanking me for coming all that way to see him, requesting I wish my daughter congratulations.

I told him I had come with my pastor – pointing to Bill – who came over and told Fernando he wasn't familiar with his music, adding that I had played him some of it in my car on the way to see him and that his voice was "perfect."

I asked Fernando if it was all right if Bill took a picture of us. He graciously consented and I still have that picture.

Upon exiting the bookstore on the way to the car, I told Bill most energetically, "We did it!"

When I recently heard Fernando Ortega on my car radio's southern gospel music station, my thoughts went back to that day Bill and I met him in Syracuse. Even though I never heard from Fernando after seeing him that day, it was an exciting experience, and that my pastor came with me, warms my heart to this day.

You want a real treat? On your computer, google, "YouTube, I Will Praise Him Still, Fernando Ortega." There are several versions to choose from, the one showing a dock amidst water is stirring to see and to listen to. I can't stress enough for you to check it out.

I Wonder, Wonder, Wonder

April 20, 2011

It's that wondering thing again. I think I do too much of it. Maybe not, though.

Let's see … I wonder if North Korea is one day going to invade South Korea, and if you have a Hyundai vehicle made in South Korea, you suddenly won't be able to get parts because they're "banging" each other good over there.

Is the sky above the clouds precisely a color of blue that never wavers?

Some years ago on that incredibly steep Vickerman Hill Road outside of Utica in Mohawk – they have yet to figure out how a field on the side of it was cut out perfectly with some kind of pattern and it's still a mystery how that happened. Like an alien type thing. I was around when it happened and passed that field on several occasions. No grass was pressed down around it to get in or out by whoever did it. Now that just doesn't compute. A practical joke? Fine, but how? Wondering had me and others thinking a lot about that.

I wonder what it would be like to fly like a bird? Wouldn't that be something?

I wonder what it would be like to be in heaven? It sounds like heaven.

What it would be like if you could sit on a cloud, or better yet, lie down on one? I know you can't do that, but what if you could?

What riding in a gondola with my wife in Venice would be like? That would be easy to find out. All I'd have to do is just write out a check.

What never having to worry about my children would be like?

What it would be like to have a private conversation with:
Elvis
Mother Teresa
Abe Lincoln
Bobby Kennedy
Jesus
Einstein
Superman
Paul McCartney
Burt Lancaster
Bugs Bunny
I wonder what it would be like to hang glide? I'm sensing terrific. Probably should wear a sweater guessing it gets cold "up there"?

I wonder what Tahiti is like? I hear that on certain beaches there, they don't wear bathing suits. I just wouldn't go to those places. Unless I swam at three in the morning when you would think no one was around. But who can stay up that late?

Wondering – it can really take you anywhere.

I wonder about – like the heaven thing – what age would you be "up there"?

Guess I'll have to wait to find out. That is, if I pass the audition.

Let Me Explain, Officer

November 16, 2011

Knowing I was to sing a solo for the first Sunday service, I went over to the church the previous evening to set up the microphone and levels for the sound system.

When I went there, the sanctuary was being used by the youth. My only choice was to get in early the next morning, before everybody else.

That night I went to sleep extra early, and got up extra early. Like one thirty in the morning. Into my mind entered, "Go over to the church now and with the key my wife has, set it up."

Deciding to do that, I went to our upstairs bathroom where I had my clothes laid out for the next morning. Also, there, was the hamper containing the clothes I wore the previous day.

My two choices: Wear the clothes from the previous day, or, wear the fresh new clothes for later that morning.

Figuring I wouldn't see anybody at that preposterous hour of the morning, I chose to wear the clothes from the previous day, with one exception. To get to the belt that was on the pants I'd wear to church, it seemed too much trouble, so I just took the chance that yesterday's pants without the belt, would hold up with a little help from my hands if need be.

I slipped out of the house driving over to the church, passing the hotel in the middle of town whose bar was still open. Looking at my watch it read 1:50 a.m.

It took me a few "go rounds" with the key to finally get the church door open, grateful no police car came accompanied with a shout of, "Against the wall, Bud!"

If that happened, I thought, "No officer, you see I go to this church. I'm just going in to set up the microphone and volume levels for the song I'm going to sing in a little over six hours."

"But officer, I beg to differ, it's not "a likely story", what do you think, I'm here to steal some cookie dough from the refrigerator? Heh, heh …"

"OK officer, so it's not funny."

But fortunately, that scenario was only in my mind.

When inside, I set up the microphone for the piano and most importantly did not hear a loud speaker from outside bellow, "You're surrounded, come on out with your hands up!"

When back in my car to drive home, a male opera singer was wailing his head off on the radio. I lunged at the volume button fearing I'd wake up the neighbors.

So what did I learn from that early hour experience?

Always wear a belt no matter the hour of the day.

Why?

For the following possibility: "But Officer, as you can see, I have no belt on, so if I don't keep hanging on to my pants, they'll fall down. Honest!"

"Hold up both my hands? Do I have to? They'll fall down… Oh all right."

"Now look at what you made me do, see – I told ya!"

I've Heard Everything

January 18, 2012

What better gift could I have received than to have seen my old friend Casabubu the day before Christmas?

Of course, I greeted him with my very best, "Merry Christmas," and what do you think his response was?

"Bah-ree, you crazy fool, tis good to see you, but I gotta ask you an important question ... to get your opinion on something that's been driving me a bit wunkys."

So I bravely asked what was on his mind.

"I saw in the Utica paper yesterday an article on what happened in the Rochester area. And I can't believe what I read."

He had my attention by that time so I anxiously waited to hear what he was so concerned about.

"Seems like a drunken man struck a deer with his vehicle."

I told Casabubu that the fact the man was drunk probably dictated why he did what he did.

"You know, Bah-ree," he said, "Sometimes you act like you got half ah brain in your head and I gotta tell you, this is one of those rare instances."

I told Casabubu hesitatingly, that I appreciated what I'd loosely refer to as a compliment from him.

He then went on to inform me that the tipsy Rochester guy then argued with his friends about what to do with the stricken deer. The reveler then decided that the deer was not dead, and needed to go to a hospital.

Casabubu continued, "So they put the sick deer in the trunk and headed for the hospital."

I told Casabubu at that point of the story, that I found it incredible to believe – tipsy or not – that they decided to take the deer to a hospital.

"You know Bah-ree, there's hope for you. Like right now you could pass 6th grade if they gave you ah test."

"Gosh, thanks," I responded.

There was no stopping Casabubu as he passionately continued relaying the story. "On the way to the hospital, with the deer in the trunk, a police officer pulled the car over and what do you think they found in the trunk?"

I took a chance and responded, "The hit deer?"

"Close, except for one minor detail," Casabubu declared.

I gave in and said, "OK what did they find?"

He declared, "The deer in the trunk was dead."

I tried injecting some humor into the conversation responding, "Are you going to tell me they had a funeral for Deersy?"

"Bah-ree, I take back what I said about you being able to pass 6th grade. If you tried, you couldn't pass the men's room."

I didn't want to respond for various reasons – recognizing it wasn't a compliment.

I wished Casabubu a Merry Christmas and even a Happy New Year, and as we parted, he said, "Bah-ree, I do love you. But you got a missing screw der in your head … you better put an ad in the paper for it and hope someone finds it."

I'm So Glad I Asked

September 5, 2012

I had to take my wife's vehicle to Utica recently to one of the big car agencies to have its oil changed and to check out why a light on the dashboard came on and off. As the gentleman took all the details of what was to be done, he had to go to the vehicle to get some information. When he got up from behind his desk to do that, he used a cane and limped.

When I was an aspiring actor in New York, I bought a book on an actor I held in the highest esteem. The book was an early collector's item which led me to believe it was pretty authentic. The book was about James Dean, who stopped me in my life tracks back in my high school days after seeing him in the film, *Rebel Without a Cause* at the gorgeous Stanley Theatre in Utica.

Very few pictures have hit me to the core as that one did. And then for humanity to lose him in a fiery car crash, well, it was most, most sad.

In that book on James's life, it told of how he would approach people on the New York streets, people who appeared to be physically life-challenged. James would talk to them, asking them about their malady. And none of them were put off by his wanting to know such sensitive information. He would go right to the source where most would shy away to avoid those delicate situations.

When I read it way back in those New York days, I thought that I should act the same if given the opportunity.

So, when the automotive check-in guy returned to where I was sitting in front of his desk and sat down, I asked him, "What happened? Why do you limp?"

One word came out of his mouth – "Afghanistan."

He told me he was in a truck with his fellow soldiers when it ran over two enemy sensors in the ground, setting off an explosion. He said he was just grateful to be alive because only seven of his buddies made it.

He said he's been in and out of hospitals since that tragedy, had been seen by many doctors, but as of yet, none of them could tell him why, when he walks, he described, "It's as if when I take a step, a knife is being stabbed in my leg." He further explained again that he was grateful to be alive and that the pain he experiences he accepts and lives with.

I asked him if he was married, and if so, did he have any children. He said he was and had a 3-year-old daughter that made everything worthwhile.

When I left him, I shook his hand and told him all free people all over the world were appreciative of his heroic efforts and that it was an honor to meet him.

I met a true hero.

Write a What?

August 22, 2012

For some time now, particularly when I've told someone a story of something out of my past, I've been asked, "Why don't you write a book?"

It's something I never really thought about. I've heard that suggestion for a number of years, but what got my attention was several people within a short period of time suggested it. I figured that was some kind of a sign that prompted me to think more seriously about it.

Write a book?

On what?

Then it occurred to me that I've already sort of done it, with these columns, so all I would have to do is some editing and put them out in book form.

Easy. Nothing to it. The columns have been written, piece of cake. Right?

Ahhhh.....as Casabubu would say, "I donno bow dat."

Speaking of Casabubu, he and I were discussing this very topic recently.

"Bah-ree what is this ting about you putting out ah book with your columns?"

I told him I was well into it and was in the final phase of editing the columns that those interested will be able to acquire in iPad, Kindle and NOOK formats, as well as paperback.

"Are you including all your *Boonville Herald* columns in this book of yours?"

I explained to him that I was only including what I perceived to be the best of those I've written since beginning them in 2002.

"So besides your wife, son and daughter, whom you'll probably charge for the books, who else will buy it?"

"There were various directions I could go in to promote it," I patiently explained. I further told him that the omnipotent publishing companies who for so long have controlled the literary market, have frustrated authors whose chances of getting publishers just to read their writing, much less publish it, was next to impossible. But the current hope with writers, is now they can have their books downloaded online, thus bypassing publishers, which is what I'm setting up with iPad, Kindle and NOOK.

"How does the public know enough about your book to, if interested, get it, "Thimble Brain?"

I told him it all goes back to promotion I was looking into. I also told him word-of-mouth and the social media, i.e. Facebook, Twitter, etc. can be most helpful. And if all else fails, they can go to BarryDamsky.com. where they can acquire the book in electronic and/or paperback form.

"You got ah better chance of winning the lottery than your book becoming successful that way."

"Casabubu, if I don't try, how am I going to know it won't work?" I asked him.

"You could try digging for diamonds in your backyard, too!" he bellowed.

"Oh", he said, in parting. "What's the name of this masterpiece of yours going to be?"

I told him, "It's going to be called, *The Peas Were Cold*."

Before driving off, he shouted, "I love you, but you're like a pistachio nut."

"How's that?" I asked, waiting for the bomb.

"You're cracked!"

Epilogue

So you now have a glimpse into a life thus far that is still reaching, hopefully more than ever.

I'm a firm believer that the best is yet to come. That all the years I've been writing, all the years I put myself "out there" for whatever dream I had at the time, that through it all, one of those would "break through", that I'd enter the big-time mainstream of whatever destiny said yes to. Along the way, trying to enjoy every minute of it.

Will *"The Peas Were Cold"* "make it"? Will my whole life culminate for that hopeful possibility?

You are the answer to that question. You who are reading this. For if you like it, somehow it will get back to me via some door being open I'll with passion walk through. In any event, hopefully I'll keep on writing, singing, performing, recording and who knows what else.

Whether you'll participate in reading my future "stuff", or listening to my music, or perhaps to even viewing it, is completely up to you.

Most sincerely, thanks for checking this out.

Sure hope you enjoyed it.

From the bottom of my heart, I hope we meet again.

Above all, Godspeed!

About the Author

Barry Damsky was born and raised in Utica, New York. His life journey took him to New York City, where he started in the mailroom of the Ashley-Famous Agency and became a television agent. His next quest was as an aspiring actor in New York for five years before relocating to Los Angeles, opening his own theatrical agency, The Barry Damsky Agency. He subsequently moved back east to his roots, ending up in Boonville, New York, near Utica, working in radio. He was the co-owner of Carpenter & Damsky Advertising in Utica. Barry was a columnist for the weekly upstate New York newspaper, the *Boonville Herald* from 2002 to 2013. His lifelong passion – in addition to writing – is singing and songwriting, with his first CD, *We Declare*, released in 2008. He is creating his second CD, *Marching On The King's Highway*. That's just the tip of Barry's iceberg. He has two children and lives in Boonville with his wife.